In response to SMALL VOICES

"In a time when the world is subjected to so much garbage (some of it literal), it is most refreshing to know there are men with wholesome values, willing to share them."

—Mary Helen Wilson

"...once I started reading, I couldn't put it down. Thank you so much for sharing your family with me."

—Dorothy Ryan

"...THANK YOU FOR WRITING THIS..."

—Lloyd Waite

SMALL VOICES

HERALDS OF WONDER
IN EVERYDAY LIFE

JIM APEL

SPARROW PRESS
Center 3000, Suite 239
3000 United Founders Blvd.
Oklahoma City, OK 73112

Library of Congress Catalog Card Number: 94-68164

Apel, James M.
    Small Voices: Heralds of Wonder in Everyday Life

ISBN 0-9642782-9-4

Manufactured in the United States

For Janel
who opened my eyes

won•der \ *n*   **1 a:** cause of astonishment or admiration: MARVEL **b:** MIRACLE **2:** astonishment at something awesomely mysterious

Contents

To the reader 11

True miracles can't be planned 15
I'll always hold your hand 21
Of teddy bears, toys and sleeping boys . . . 25
❖
What's really important in life? 31
I'll do Jane 35
You're in the army now 39
Grandpa's hat 43
Can I be a grandma instead? 49
The best Christmas 53
❖
I'm tired of being afraid 61
Dancer of the heart 65
Seeds of future harvests 69
Kiss it all better 73
I'm not a wise man anymore 77
❖
Things that go bump in the night 85
Angry eyes 89
The priceless gift of life 93
Land the plane now 97
We'll make it somehow 101
Gold medal all the way 105
What's it going to hurt? 109
I've been down that road 113

I want to be in your picture, Em 117
Home is where the neighbors are 121
A father's tears 125
Unfinished business 129
He's my hero 133
To hell in a handbasket 137
An apple for the teacher 141
A camcorderless Christmas 145
Happy birthday to us 149
Grandpa Elmer's bequest 153
❖
True professionals 159
Don't tell them I can fly 163
Politicians just don't get it 167
Hold you in my arms 171
A $500 lesson worth every penny 175
I'd love to go to lunch, but... 179
❖
All the world needs a waver 185
TV can do without me 189
The road not taken 193
True home improvements 197
Bless me with a lullaby 201

To the reader

This book simply came to be to fulfill readers' kind requests for reprints of a syndicated weekly column I write for small town newspapers. The column, and the stories collected herein, are about discovering snippets of wonder that permeate our everyday lives although we often find ourselves too busy, too serious, or just plain too tired to look.

With the birth of our first child six years ago, it was as if someone turned on a type of hearing aid for me, an aid with which to experience life on a level more satisfying than anything I'd previously known. Since that time I've held my tongue more, listened when I would rather have talked, and I've been amazed at what I've learned. God speaks. He does. And he seems to do so most often using the voices of small children immersed in seemingly coincidental, ordinary activities of family life.

I began committing some of these experiences to

paper against the day my mind would fail (some would say it already has) and all my learning would account for naught. I wanted to let my family and friends know, somehow, what I'd learned about life with their help.

A friend read one of the stories I'd left sitting on my desk one day and asked if he could begin publishing them as a regular column in his newspaper. Other newspapers followed suit and rare has been the week since that has not brought with it kind letters or calls from readers across the country relating their own heartwarming stories of wonders discovered.

With that in mind, I ask you to read this book slowly. If you find stories of your own coming to mind, so be it. Simply close the book, set it aside and let your own memories take hold. Cherish them as the priceless gifts that they are. Don't be afraid to let them prompt you to laughter or move you to tears. And don't be surprised when you discover, in the whirl of events crowding your own busy life, that God has been speaking to you all along, too.

SMALL VOICES

True miracles can't be planned

I stared for what seemed to be a long time at the empty place my wife's hospital bed had occupied just moments before. Something inside told me I was entitled to collapse in a sobbing heap at a time like this, but I couldn't. Alone and emotionally numbed in this now-deserted birthing suite, I wanted to deny for a while longer the fact that the miracle Janel and I had hoped for, prayed for, and planned for was not going to happen. Having been tersely ordered by a nurse to stay put until I was called, I slumped into a chair in the corner incredulous at how rapidly the prospect of new life can turn toward death. As the silence of this empty room pressed in, tears started to come.

It had been just past midnight when Nel had crawled back into our bed at home after one of her frequent ninth-month trips to the bathroom.

"Jim, the water's broken," she had said.

Our home's well pump had been sounding like it

was on its last legs for months and I mumbled something like "I'll fix it later," without opening my eyes.

Taking my wrist, Janel placed my hand on a wet spot on the sheet where *her* water had broken.

My eyes now wide open, I could see a radiant smile lighting her face in the twilight.

Unlike the stereotypical, chaotic, slapstick dash first-time mothers and fathers are supposed to make to the hospital, Janel and I showered and dressed leisurely and drove the four miles to the hospital. She said her pains weren't too severe and finally went away altogether. She slept soundly in her hospital bed while I tossed and turned in a chair.

Late in the morning, since the labor pains had not returned, the doctor ordered an intravenous drip of pitocyn, a hormone to help stimulate the stalled delivery. The nurses simply called it "Pit."

How appropriate. Almost immediately Nel was wracked with intense contractions that left her speechless.

About noon a nurse pushing a cart full of electrical equipment came to hook the baby up to a monitor of its own. Janel and I had discussed this possibility weeks earlier when it had been explained to us during childbirth class. We had decided we'd rather not have it done if it weren't an absolute emergency. The nurse didn't even look in my direction let alone ask our permission before going about her business.

"Doctor's orders," was all she said to Janel.

I was beginning to feel more and more like an observer and less and less like the participating father I'd been led to believe during classes I was needed to be.

Our two-person team was disintegrating.

During her ordeal, Nel never cried out nor asked for pain medication, although on numerous occasions I was ready to ask; with each pitocyn-induced contraction she would squeeze my hand painfully with all her strength.

By mid-afternoon still no baby had come and Nel fell into 30- to 45-second snippets of sleep between contractions. It was clear she couldn't go on like this much longer. During one particularly rough contraction, sweat beaded on her forehead and her gaze became far away and unfocused. Something was definitely wrong.

I reassured Nel softly, hoping she couldn't sense the tide of fear rising deep inside me.

Without a word, a nurse watching the baby's heartbeat monitor ran from the room and returned with an oxygen mask for Janel.

A minute later a doctor rushed in, took one look at the monitor and, looking past me as if I weren't even there, told Nel that the baby was in trouble and emergency surgery was necessary.

Moments later, gowned and masked orderlies swooped in and Nel was gone. I was alone in that empty delivery room. No wife, no baby.

Now I was really afraid.

My voice cracking, I phoned our pastor and asked for the church's prayers. I put the phone down and stood there, dazed, before slumping into a chair.

It couldn't have been more than a few of minutes before a nurse came and led me by the hand to the elevator out in the hall. From somewhere below I could hear the muffled cries of a baby drifting up through the elevator shaft. Nurses gathered around. When the door opened, a nurse in a scrub suit handed me the bundled up baby and over its screams said, "He's a nice, healthy baby boy.

"Mama's fine," she added before the elevator door abruptly shut, cutting us off.

Not sure what to do, I just stood there cradling that bundle for all I was worth.

The nurses' congratulations were still ringing in my ears when I noticed they had all gone. This baby boy, for whom we had not yet settled on a name, and I were left all alone in that hallway. Childbirth classes had done nothing to prepare me for this.

At that moment I missed Janel more than I had ever missed her in our fourteen months of marriage. I so longed for her to be with us and share these first few miraculous moments of life like we had planned.

I gloried in our baby's handsome face and shock of thick, black hair through my tear-filled eyes, my hands rubbing his back. To my surprise, his crying stopped.

Mine didn't, for at that moment I recalled that if everything had truly gone as planned, I wouldn't have been here even for this. When Nel went into labor I would have been hundreds of miles away sleeping in our new home—a home that did not yet have a telephone—resting up for another day on the new job I'd just taken to support this growing family. The fact that I hadn't been sleepy earlier in the evening and had driven home unexpectedly to haul yet another load of our belongings to our new home had simply been a coincidence.

Or had it?

I don't know how long the baby and I had been standing there in the hospital hallway when, through my tears, I caught sight of a nurse peering at us through the nursery doorway watching this new life and I get acquainted. As if she could sense my embarrassment, she smiled, winked and nodded once as if to say, "Quite a miracle, isn't it?"

If only she knew. Without a doubt, it most certainly was.

I'll always hold your hand

For my first official Father's Day, Matthew made a card for me. That's quite an accomplishment considering he was four days shy of being a full four months old at the time. Janel finally confessed that she had helped, but she insisted it was all Matthew's idea.

On the outside of the oversized card is a series of Matthew's footprints in green fingerpaint. The part Nel said he needed help with was the lettering. On the front it says: "Papa, I may never be able to walk in your footsteps..."

On the inside are Matthew's handprints in the same green paint. Beside them the verse continues: "...but I know you'll always be there to hold my hand and guide me."

I cut the card apart and framed it so both the inside and the outside show at the same time. I hung it in my office. Now and then it will catch

my eye, especially on days when I'm full of
myself and sitting high on a pedestal looking
down my nose at the rest of humanity. The
message can still bring me to tears.

As my mother taught me to do when I was a
child (although, ashamedly, I admit having ne-
glected this particular lesson quite often since
then), I decided to write Matthew a letter thank-
ing him for his gift:

Dearest Matthew,
Thank you for the nice Father's Day card. The
size of your feet and hands is misleading. Your
heart is already so much bigger than they. I
thank God for blessing me with a child as thought-
ful as you.

If you'd like, I'd love to have you follow in my
footsteps. What father wouldn't? But if you
choose not to follow them, I hope it is because
my strides are much too short for you. As you
grow in wisdom I'd hate for you to slow down just
to be polite and follow my lead. Besides, my
steps have traced a path that's a series of fits
and starts that doubles back on itself time and
again. I've made plenty of mistakes in my life
and I'd hate for you to make the same ones all
over again by blindly following along. The best
I can hope is that when the time comes for you

to make decisions, I'll be able to listen with an open heart and optimistically accept your choices even though they may differ from my own.

Do not be afraid to set your own course, Matthew. All I ask as your father is that you be kind when you decide your steps must veer from mine. And, please, don't burn your bridges behind you. You can never tell when you might want to come home again or when you'll want me to come visit you.

"I know you'll always be there to hold my hand and guide me," your card says. That line haunts me. Life is so fragile. None of us knows when it is time to die. I've already come closer than I want. I don't know how long I'll be here with you and I'm not sure sometimes what guidance I have to offer. There are some times when I don't even know if I'm grown up yet, but I will do my best. And I promise you, Matthew, for as long as you'll let me, I will hold your hand. To the barn. To the zoo. To the doctor. To the schoolyard on your first day of school. When it's dark. When you're afraid. When I'm afraid. I will be there to hold your hand.

When we hold hands we're a team. Neither one leads, neither one follows. We're fellow adventurers on a journey. Right now your steps are unsteady and need my support. You seek my hand instinctively. I take that responsibility very seriously. Someday, though, it will be different. You will be strong and tall and I will be weak and tired. But when you ask, I will let go. It won't be easy, but it must be that way. I think that's what being a father is all about.

For now, though, I want to be your friend so bad I can taste it, Matthew. Perhaps that's the best guidance I have to offer—let's make the most of being friends, you and I.

In your brief lifetime you've already come a long way. With God's blessing, we have a long way yet to go. Let's see where, and for how long, that path will lead us together.

I'll love you always,
Papa

Of teddy bears, toys and sleeping boys

It was about three o'clock in the morning when I finally gave up working on the second edition of a small newspaper I had started when Matthew was nine months old. There were mounds of work left to do, but I just couldn't go on. The computer was giving me fits and my eyes were finding it hard to focus. I'd had less than ten hours of sleep total in the previous three days. Exhausted and frustrated that I couldn't go on, I crept as quietly as I could down the stairs, but it was hard to avoid clomp-clomping down the low, narrow wooden stairway in that eighty-year-old farmhouse. Janel told me once I sounded like a one-legged pirate.

Not this night. Nel was fast asleep on her side of the bed and Annah, our Doberman pinscher, was asleep under a blanket on the floor next to her. Neither of them stirred as I passed.

Matthew's bedroom adjoined ours, and through

the open door I could hear him restlessly tossing in his crib.

I stopped in midstride lest the creaking floorboards beneath the worn, rose-patterned carpet awaken him completely. He had been teething and hadn't been sleeping well. The last thing I needed that night was a crying baby to contend with.

In a few seconds he settled down and his breathing became slow and even like it usually did when he slept. I slipped my tennis shoes off and crawled under the covers still dressed. I had to get up in a couple of hours to finish laying out the paper before the printer's deadline.

The warmth of the waterbed was soothing to my tired back, but my mind remained a restless jumble of thoughts. Emotionally, I couldn't get comfortable. Sleep wouldn't come. I laid there for about thirty minutes, the alarm clock ticking away on the headboard above my right ear.

Tired though I was, something prodded me to get up and steal into Matthew's room. It was like an unheard voice softly calling my name. I tiptoed in and on the way picked up a quilt from the chair next to the door. The quilt blocks had been hand embroidered by Janel's friends at the animal clinic where she worked up until the week Matthew was born. I settled quietly into the big easy chair she had placed next to Matthew's bed to rock him to sleep in on restless nights.

Maybe it would work for me.

Thoughts of the looming deadline and nagging questions churned my stomach. What if I missed the deadline? Could the printer reschedule me later in the day? Why did I start a newspaper without adequate help anyway? Was this half-baked endeavor really in the best interests of my family? Wouldn't it be easier just to forget it all and concentrate on my day job as a college journalism teacher instead?

I just sat there in Matthew's room. Through the window the remaining slender crescent moon shed little light.

In the silence, all I could hear was Matthew's breathing. His peaceful respiration seemed like music when compared to my own choppy, shallow breaths. My breathing was about as troubled as my mind.

Ever so slowly, one by one, the little voices in my head fell silent. It was then that I noticed a funny thing happening. The longer I sat there next to Matthew the easier my breathing became. I rocked slowly in the easy chair, careful not to let it squeak. Before long my mind was clear and I thought I was ready for bed. But, surprisingly, now I didn't want to go.

There was something so powerfully magnetic

about the humble, innocent calm that perfused this little room full of teddy bears, toys, and a peacefully sleeping infant boy—a feeling so absolutely foreign to the upstairs office that I had let claim so much of my recent life.

As I rocked gently in that peaceful place, it slowly became clear that my desire to prove myself as an editor to a town full of people whom I did not know was utterly unfair to the house full of people whom I did know.   I had unwisely burdened myself with a workload that I could not possibly shoulder and still raise the kind of family I knew in my heart I was called to raise.

As much as it hurt to let go of the dream, I resolved then and there, in the quiet presence of my sleeping first-born son and his legion of teddy bears as witnesses, to fold the newspaper after the current issue was completed.

Mysteriously lightened of my burden, I found myself rising from the chair, blowing Matthew a kiss and tousling his hair gently, much as I remember my father tousling mine in his appreciative way many years before.

"Thanks, Matthew," I whispered. "I owe you one. I love you. Goodnight."

What's really important in life?

As the sun set, casting its pinkish-orange glow through our west windows one evening, our canary started singing. It wasn't unusual for her to sing in the evening, but I usually wasn't home to hear her. Or if I was, my mind was usually not there to notice—I'd be off in La La Land somewhere still mulling over some trivial office problem or the deadline for some unfinished writing assignment.

Such was the case that evening as we sat eating dinner in the kitchen when two-year-old Matthew called my attention to her singing.

"Papa? Hear the bird?"

I pretended to listen for a second. "Yeah, Matthew. Now eat your dinner like a big guy," I said, going back to my own big-guy meat-and-potatoes dinner.

In reality, I tried not to hear. The canary shared her tiny cage with a green parakeet and

31

I felt a bit guilty. I'd been planning to build them a new cage ever since we moved into this house over a year ago, but I'd never gotten around to it.

"Bird singing, Papa," Matthew said matter-of-factly again, a smidgeon of mashed potatoes stuck to his chin. He sat with his head cocked, a toothy grin lighting his face, listening intently as his dinner grew colder. "Bird singing, 'I love my life, I love my life.'"

I hacked away at my overdone pork chop.

"Listen, Papa," Matthew commanded. "'I love my life, I love my life,' bird singing."

Quite an imagination, I thought, playing along for a second before retreating into my own thoughts.

Nel accused me of walling her out and I couldn't deny it, but she was only half right. I'd walled myself in. I was like the tiger at the Oklahoma City Zoo that paces back and forth, back and forth, restless in its tiny enclosure. It was nothing big really. I was just wrestling with some of the silly problems that plagued my life that day:

—I wasn't too happy with the fact that I'd be driving to school the following evening. I drove back and forth to graduate classes in Edmond, Oklahoma, from our farm in Capron, Oklahoma, two nights a week to the tune of 600 miles per week all while trying to juggle a full-time job and a full-time family.

—Our beat up silver station wagon had turned 150,000 on the way home from church the week before. My red Yugo's odometer had just clicked off 63,000 miles and it collected an extra 700-plus each week. Does anyone know how long a Yugo will last?

—My shoes had just about given up the ghost. They didn't look too bad on the outside, at least they didn't have any holes yet, but the arch support and insoles were shot. A hundred dollars seemed like an awful lot of money to spend on one pair of shoes. Nel had found a couple of pairs on sale for Matthew a few days earlier for $2.50 a pair. It made infinitely more sense to buy forty pairs in assorted sizes for him and his newborn sister, Emily, to grow through than it did to buy a single pair in my size.

In bed later that night, I tossed and turned. Work and unfinished homework kept creeping in. A nagging thought just wouldn't go away: What's really important in life?

I didn't find any convincing answers as the alarm clock mockingly ticked away each passing second before I finally dozed off.

While I was shaving the next morning I spent a few moments in my mind playing with Matthew and Emily. It saddened me that I would be on my way to work before they were even out of bed, but the memories of our shared time on the weekends brightened my mood. As the sky outside the bathroom window began to lighten, it occurred to me that maybe we as parents aren't given kids just so we can teach and protect them. Maybe we are given kids to help bring us back to what's really important in life.

And, frankly, as I recalled the concerns that had occupied my mind the previous day, most of my problems weren't very important at all.

For some reason I went out the front door that morning instead of the back. Just as I passed the bird cage outside of Matthew's and Emily's room both the parakeet and the canary started to sing.

I'll be derned—they were both chirping the same tune: "I love my life, I love my life…"

I'll do Jane

Twenty minutes' worth of hot shower massage on my lower back before work one morning had done nothing to ease the pain.

"I'll get you for this, Jane," I groaned, lying on the bed struggling to pull on my socks without bending my back.

"What did you say?" Nel mumbled, more asleep than awake.

"Oh, nothing," I lied, holding a sock between the tips of my index and middle fingers, attempting to flip its opening over my left big toe. The purposely exaggerated grunts and groans of my repeated efforts elicited no further response from my wife.

She had fallen blissfully back to sleep.

I wanted to shake her awake. I wanted her to share my agony. My back problem was as much her fault as it was Jane Fonda's.

If I didn't know better, I'd say that when Nel heard my car drive in a little early the previous afternoon she had jumped off the couch, turned off the soap opera, slipped Jane Fonda's workout video into the player, and pretended she was nearing the end of a workout when I walked through the door.

"Shhh," she said from her yoga-like position on the floor, "the kids are sleeping." She was lying on her side, one leg bent in front of her like a pretzel, the other one pointed crazily at the ceiling. "Join me?" she invited.

"Yeah, right." I slumped into the recliner.

"Come on. It's not hard."

After more of her cajoling, I finally went limp, sliding onto the floor like an octupus I'd seen escape from an aquarium on a Jaques Cousteau special once. "There. I'm done."

"Come on," Nel goaded.

I folded myself into the pretzel position and began wagging my arms and legs like they were doing on the screen. I could feel muscles stretch that most likely hadn't been stretched since junior high during one of the sadistic calisthenic marathons Mr. Hardridge called gym class.

"Doesn't that feel good?" Jane questioned seductively from her own pretzel position on the screen.

Get real, Jane. After about thirty seconds of torture I quit, collapsing in a heap. "I can't do it Nel. I'm just too old," I joked.

The video ended and Janel got up seemingly refreshed. "If you'd do that every day," she said standing over me, "you'd live longer and feel younger. You'd be surprised."

Yeah. And in traction. Which, as I drove to work the next morning, was sounding like a pretty good place to be. Every bump in the road shot spasms of pain up my back. After one especially nasty jolt about two miles from home, cursing, I swore off exercise as well as Jane Fonda movies for good. No more *Electric Horseman* for me.

A couple of miles further on, the glint of sunlight off a new swing set in a neighbor's backyard caught my eye. Strange. The neighbors were both retired. Then it hit me—grandkids.

Automatically a string of calculations ran through my head. Let's see, if Matthew and Emily wait to have kids as long as I did, it will most likely be a couple of decades into the next century before I'll be a grandfather. I found myself saddened that it would be so long. Despite that cold realization, a warm feeling came over me—I'd just discovered that I was looking forward to being older. I'd never given it much thought before. Actually, I'd never contemplated making it that far.

As the fence posts rushed by and the new swing set receded in the rearview mirror, I thought about the hours I'd spent on the swing in my backyard as a kid. A twinge of pain hit me, but this time it wasn't my back. It hit a little higher and a little deeper—most of my hours on the swing set were spent alone—I'd never had a grandpa to push me. I'd never shared the satisfied laughter of swinging with a playful old man on a crisp fall afternoon. My father's dad had died when Dad was a young boy. My mother's father had been an invalid all the time I'd known him until he died when I was a teenager.

As I drove along that morning I recalled the lonely creaking sounds our old swings' chains made in their hooks on the crossbar. I'd truly missed one of life's most pleasant treats.

When I pulled into the parking lot a little while later I turned the car off and sat for a moment. As I watched college students rush by on their way to class, I found within myself a burgeoning desire to live as long as possible so my future grandkids won't have to miss out—not if I have anything to say about it.

Move over, Nel. I'll do Jane. For them.

You're in the army now

A short nap was all I wanted when I lay down on the living room carpet beneath the whirling ceiling fan one August afternoon. An all-day, 320-mile round trip from the farm to Oklahoma City and back in my unairconditioned Yugo had sapped my energy.

On the road, I had ached for details of the then escalating American troop deployment to the Persian Gulf. Before each newscast I had found myself hoping they would announce shooting had started. After all, I reasoned, the Kuwaitis needed us.

It must be some kind of radar two-year-olds have that alerts them when a nearby adult is getting any kind of rest. Mine plopped his little behind on a small wicker chair he'd carried in from his room, grabbed my hand and began tugging.

"Papa, let's play."

"Let Papa have just a little nap, Matthew. I'll play with you after dinner. I promise."

"Come on, Papa. Play now."

"I'm old and tired, Matthew," I groaned, hoping he wouldn't remember my words to use against me in a few years. "Let me sleep just a few minutes."

He didn't answer me, but he began playing by himself with a little army truck he'd picked up from the floor.

As I was drifting somewhere between consciousness and sleep, Matthew reached over, touched my forehead and said, "Peace be with you, Papa," repeating the little ritual the members of our family share every night before we go to bed.

Moments later I could have sworn I felt a much stronger hand shaking my shoulder. "Papa. Papa, wake up. I've got to go."

Through sleep-bleary eyes I could barely make out the face of a nineteen-year-old boy. I had never seen this nineteen-year-old face before, but there was no question in my mind who it belonged to. It was the first time I had ever seen Matthew in a GI haircut.

An unbuttoned desert camouflage blouse revealed a shiny pair of dog tags dangling from a chain around his neck. The low rumble of an idling engine out near the road drifted in with the breeze through the window screen.

The boy hurriedly pulled on a pair of combat boots, slung an M-16 over his shoulder and headed for the door. I followed, but stayed on the porch as he loped down the dirt drive toward an open-sided army truck parked on the road. It was nearly full of boys about his same age buttoning fatigues, lacing boots and assembling rifles.

About halfway down the drive Matthew turned toward me, walking backward without breaking stride and called, "I love you, Papa. Peace be with you."

I have no idea how long I actually slept, but when I woke up from that dream I was hotter than when I had lain down. I was sweaty all over. Matthew's little chair was empty except for the little truck he'd been playing with.

At dinner later, I didn't bother to tell Nel about my dream.

Later that night rolling booms of thunder awakened both Janel and me. I got up and began shutting windows and Nel went to check on Matthew and Emily. When she came back to bed she said that Matthew's covers were pulled up over his head and he was drenched with sweat.

"I guess he's afraid of lightning," she said.

I knew better. He's not. In fact, before going to bed, he and I had gone outside to watch the light show in the tops of the distant, approaching thunderheads.

As Janel and I lay together and the eerie shadows of lightning played across the walls, I silently prayed Matthew wasn't having the same nightmare about having to go fight a war that I'd endured earlier that afternoon. To my surprise, I also found myself praying that reason would prevail in the Gulf, that diplomacy would work, and that all the soldiers sleeping in the desert fearing a poison gas attack would return safe and whole as the little boys and girls they would always be to their parents.

As we know now, it didn't turn out that way. Families on both sides will mourn forever their little boys and girls who did not return.

The news has changed little since that time and it seems we hear of troops deploying at hot spots all across the globe. To this day, as I hope it will always remain, my prayer is the same:

Peace be with them.

Grandpa's hat

The sun had barely begun to paint its early-morning rays on the wall of our bedroom one Saturday in early fall when a small finger lifted up my eyelid. There stood two-year-old Matthew grinning broadly, a large white t-shirt swallowing his body from shoulder to knee. Tufts of hair stood up crazily in odd directions.

"Papa stay home this morning?" he questioned energetically.

"Yes, Matthew," I mumbled, my mouth sticky. "Papa stay home today." I wrapped an arm around his diapered behind and flipped him onto the bed as I rolled over, burying my face in a pillow.

"Come on, Papa," he pleaded, pulling at the pillow. "Put Matthew's shoes on. I go outside and get Matthew's tractor out of car so we can play."

I wanted to play, but I really needed to work

around the yard. The dead weeds needed mowing one last time and the overflowing trash
barrels begged to be emptied.

"Papa's got to work today."

"Papa work at home. OK?" he conceded, pointing a finger at me.

"Right," I said with a nod. "Papa will work at
home."

There was barely a pause before he continued
impatiently, "Papa, get up." He prodded until I
did finally get up and dress us both.

At breakfast I told Nel I needed to go to the
neighbor's farm and borrow his tractor with a
front-end loader.

Matthew's face brightened in anticipation. "Get
John's tractor with no windows, Papa. Matthew
want to drive," he commanded.

Matthew was in the yard waiting when I returned with the old tractor with the red primer
showing through patches in the thinning, sun-
bleached green paint. Safely inside the fence, he
followed as I eased the tractor down the drive
and around the curve to where the trash barrels
sat next to the garage.

"Papa! Papa!" he yelled, struggling to be heard
over the growl of the tractor. "Matthew's turn to
drive!"

I shut down the motor and lifted Matthew over

the fence, depositing him on the seat to drive while I dumped the trash barrels into the tractor's scoop.

I hated dumping the trash, so I usually put it off as long as I could. Driving the tractor over the rough field to empty the non-burnable trash into a landfill at the neighbors' place always scared me. I was afraid the tractor would flip over. Once started with the chore I usually hurried to get it behind me as quickly as possible.

Not today, though. As I watched Matthew plow imaginary fields from his perch on the tractor's seat, I took my time. I reached into the barrels and emptied their contents slowly instead of dumping them all at once. There was something going on here worth watching.

Matthew was oblivious of me. His eyes were fixed on some distant horizon. His bottom was planted firmly on the torn form rubber seat of the open-air John Deere tractor that was older than I was. He worked the weather-cracked steering wheel back and forth methodically as if he were trying to stay lined up on some invisible furrow. I could only imagine what fertile ground he was turning over in his head.

As he drove, I could see his lips moving. It appeared as if he were carrying on some conversation whose words I didn't understand.

He took his hands off the steering wheel just long enough to adjust his "farmer's" hat as he called it—a broken-down fedora like men wore in the 40s and 50s. It had belonged to his great grandpa.

For some reason, the more I watched Matthew the more I began to wonder what kind of magic might be contained in that hat. Could it be that, perhaps, in some mystical way, Matthew's great grandpa Wesley Rutt, who had grown up on a farm as a boy himself, was carrying on some kind of unspoken conversation with him? Maybe Matthew was refining and finishing the thoughts and daydreams Wesley had poured into that hat under the light of the same sun many years before.

It struck me as odd that none of Wesley's own children had wanted that hat, that physical touchstone to their father, after he had died in 1978. It sat in a closet gathering dust for years until Nel claimed it for Matthew when great grandma Ruth died.

As I bounced over the field a little later that morning heading for the landfill, I had no way to be certain about the thoughts that had been turning over in Matthew's head, but I did know about those turning over in my heart. There are an awful lot of things we don't know about this world; we know even less about the next. The relatives who have gone before me, those that have given me their love, are responsible for everything I have and everything I am. Now it all comes down to a boy on a tractor in the sun wearing his great grandpa's hat.

My boy. My love.

Can I be a grandma instead?

As soon as Matthew picked up the dusty peanut butter jar filled with 16-penny nails in John Scripsick's shop, in some fatherly way I just knew an accident was about to happen.

"Matthew, put the nails back," I said firmly, fearing he would drop the glass on the concrete floor and hurt himself. I would have taken the jar from him, but my hands were busy steadying two pieces of iron for John, Matthew's self-appointed surrogate grandfather, to weld.

"I'll be careful, Papa," Matthew replied, peeking at me around the glass jar containing a two-year-old's treasure.

"Matthew!" I ordered. "Put it down! That's dangerous."

He got the message that the jar was not a toy, but instead of setting it down he said, "Here, Papa. I'll bring it to you. OK?"

"No, Matthew. Just set it down."

He started threading his way through the assorted boxes, power tools, hunks of iron, and scattered tools that littered John's work area. Keeping one eye on me and one eye on the jar, Matthew didn't see the air hose from the compressor snaking across the floor.

"Matthew!" I screamed.

Too late. He looked down just as his toe caught on the yellow hose. It was as if he began to fall in slow motion, clutching the jar tighter in his hand so he wouldn't drop it, wouldn't disappoint me.

Before Matthew hit the floor, I dropped the steel shaft I was holding, nearly smashing John's toes. Before I could catch Matthew, though, the bottom edge of the jar hit the floor with a sharp pop, exploding into shards that showered him.

Spread-eagle on the grimy floor, Matthew looked up at me, his eyes wide, incredulous that I could let something like this happen. He lifted up his hand that was now running with blood and let out a wail.

Immediately I scooped him up, raised his arm above his head and ran toward the house. We burst through the back door and trailed drops of blood into the washroom where I began rinsing his hand with water. His terrified screams filled my ears. I wanted to cry, too. There was so much blood for a such a little guy.

"Hold me, Papa! Hold me!" he screamed over and over as I struggled to subdue him and assess the damage. I don't know if it were some defense mechanism kicking in, but it all became very clinical to me, like triage on an episode of *M*A*S*H*. The nasty gashes on Matthew's left ring finger and a couple of smaller ones on his pinky didn't appear to need stitches, but I couldn't tell for sure. I thought I could handle them if he would just simmer down, but no amount of reassurance or coercion on my part could stop his screaming and wriggling.

Just then John's wife (Grandma Lottie to Matthew) stepped in, deftly wrapped a washcloth around his bloody hand so he couldn't see it and swept him into her arms as if I weren't there.

"Come on, Sugar," she said calmly. "It's not so bad. Let Grandma fix you up." After a moment— and a detour to the kitchen—his crying stopped.

I drifted back out to the shop, mulling over what had just happened. One minute I'm Dr. Dad, the next minute I'm a nobody unable to even bandage my son's fingers. I picked up the shaft and John and I took up where we left off.

A little while later Lottie appeared at the shop door, bloodstains on her white blouse, Matthew in her arms, a couple of cookies in his hand.

"See, Papa," he beamed, holding up his hand to show me the bandages on his fingers. "Grandma made it all better."

I was happy he was OK, but I felt guilty for letting the accident happen in the first place. I was also sad that I hadn't been the one to make it all better.

In that uncanny way of hers, Lottie seemed to know what was going through my mind. "I'm sorry," she apologized. "That's just the way we grandmas are."

John and I kept working while Matthew resumed his workshop treasure hunt—albeit a little more carefully.

Normally talkative with John, I didn't have much to say as I turned the afternoon's events over in my mind. After a while it became clear that Lottie had been able to do what she had done because she hadn't been focusing on fixing cuts on a little person's hand. She had been ministering to a frightened little boy who was so scared because his papa had been scared. He hadn't needed doctoring so much as he had needed comfort.

So much for being Dr. Dad. Can I be a grandma instead?

The best Christmas

Our bank account had been wiped out by a couple of extra courses I'd needed to take at school earlier in the fall, and Christmas was shaping up as a big disappointment. Janel and I canceled our trip to her parents' house and dropped plans to buy much in the way of Christmas gifts for two-year-old Matthew and nine-month-old Emily. There certainly would be nothing for us.

I pouted about it for weeks. It wasn't until well before sunrise Christmas Eve morning that I finally figured out why. As I lay awake in the dark listening to the icy north wind roaring through the trees, it dawned on me. Or, rather, it dismayed me: like an immature adolescent I wanted gifts, tangible, material gifts. I could live with the fact that my kids wouldn't be getting much for Christmas, but I couldn't accept the fact that there wouldn't be much under the tree for me.

Angry with myself for being so childish, I tossed the blanket off and walked into the bathroom to get a drink. I turned on the faucet.

Nothing.

"Damn it!" I roared, waking Janel. "The water's frozen!"

Having lived on that farm in northwestern Oklahoma for a few years, it came as no surprise that the week of Christmas was usually the coldest week of the year. I had intended to put a heater out in the wellhouse, but like so many other things in my life, I simply hadn't gotten around to doing it.

I spent most of Christmas Eve outside trying desperately to thaw the pipes. I tried every trick I knew including torches, heaters and heat lamps, but the temperature inside the wellhouse never rose above twenty degrees. As it began to grow dark, in frustration, I slammed a wrench against a pipe elbow and, being so cold, the plastic fitting shattered.

I stormed into the house nearly ready to cry. "What else can I screw up this Christmas?" I fumed to Janel. "Why is this all happening to me?"

"Just calm down," she said, handing me a cup of hot chocolate. "Call Glenn. He'll know what to do."

"It's almost Christmas, Nel, or haven't you noticed?" I shot back angrily, not wanting to have to confess to Glenn that I'd broken the pipe myself in a fit of rage.

Glenn was a neighbor who lived five miles down the road. He ran the hardware store in town and was a pretty good plumber on the side.

"Take it easy, Jim. Just call him."

After I'd cooled off and warmed up a bit, I finally called and Glenn said he probably had a spare pipe elbow in his barn and he'd bring it right up.

A few minutes later his wife, Georgianna, and their two kids drove up. "Glenn had to go to town for parts," she said. "He'll be here shortly." She herded her kids toward the house before producing a large plate of cookies from her car's back seat. "Without any water, I don't imagine Janel got much Christmas baking done."

When Glenn arrived an hour later he found me down in the wellhouse staring blankly at the broken pipe.

"Why don't you let me give it a shot," he said. "You've been at it all day."

He climbed into the wellhouse and spent two hours repairing the damage I had done before he attempted to slowly thaw the pipes. Near midnight, he threw the switch on the pump and water again flowed into the house. He wrapped the pipes with insulation and turned on the heater full blast.

"That should do it," he said, climbing up out of the wellhouse and shutting the lid tightly against the biting northern gale.

His wife and kids had long since left. Glenn climbed into his pickup and waved off my offer to pay for the parts and his time. "My pleasure," he simply said. "Merry Christmas."

When I stepped into the kitchen a moment later, I could see Janel and the kids snuggled on the hide-a-bed next to the Christmas tree in the living room. Matthew lay on his back watching the twinkling lights trace patterns on the ceiling, his eyelids growing heavier with every passing moment. Janel, singing softly, cradled Emily on her chest. As I quietly stripped off my coveralls, I leaned back against the wall listening to Nel's sweet voice sing the lullaby "Baby Mine" from the movie *Dumbo*.

I lost it. Tears welled in my eyes, finally spilling over onto my cheeks. The question I'd posed to Janel earlier in the day now begged an honest answer: "Why is all this happening to me?"

How blind I had been. The gifts I had been

given this year were much too large to wrap and fit under any Christmas tree—a loving wife and devoted mother, healthy children and generous neighbors.

Through no merit of my own, money or not, in God's own wisdom, Christmas had come to the Apel house—the best Christmas of my life.

I'm tired of being afraid

"I'm showing Papa where the potty is," three-year-old Matthew announced, zig-zagging me to table after table of McDonald's diners comprising the noon crowd in the restaurant just north of Kansas City on I-35.

Embarrassed, all I could manage was a sheepish grin, admonishing Matthew that we shouldn't speak to strangers and we didn't have to announce our destination to everyone.

He gripped my fingers tighter and hauled me past the next table. "Papa has to go potty."

The lone trucker-looking diner looked at me, lowered the sandwich from his lips, and strained to stifle a snicker. He was straining so hard that for a second I thought he might force a bite of Big Mac through his nose.

Once in the restroom, thank goodness, Matthew and I were alone. No telling what he would have felt compelled to announce to someone in there.

On the way out I tried to pick him up so he wouldn't be so apt to wander embarrassingly. Matthew deftly "juked me out" as our hometown sportswriter would put it, and shot out the door. I caught up with him at an out-of-the-way table occupied by a young family about like our own. They had a young boy about Matthew's age and a small baby. Matthew's hands gripped the edge of the table, his eyes peering over them at the baby breastfeeding in its mother's arms.

I caught him by the shoulders and tried to lead him away. "Come on, Matthew. Let's let these people eat."

He looked up at the young father and said, "My papa was a good boy. He went potty."

Instead of nodding politely or averting his gaze, the young man looked up at me, compounding my distress. "Cute boy. He's so outgoing. I bet you're really proud of him."

The comment startled me. As I thought about it for a moment, unfortunately, I couldn't answer in the affirmative. Red faced and embarrassed for myself, it hadn't even occurred to me to feel proud of my son's desire to speak to others.

On the road north that afternoon, passing through Missouri, Iowa, and then into Illinois, with Janel and the kids napping in their seats, the McDonald's incident floated in and out of my thoughts before slowly drifting away.

A couple of days later on a sidewalk in front of a supermarket in my in-laws' hometown of Dixon, Illinois, while we waited for the rain to subside before dashing to our van, Matthew reached his hand out toward a woman about to step off the curb. "Hold my hand so you don't get hit by a car," he piped up.

The woman looked at him quizzically and stepped off the curb anyway.

"How come she didn't hold my hand, Papa?" Matthew asked.

"I think she's afraid," I found myself blurting out in explanation before I'd really even thought about it.

Later that afternoon, walking in a park in Sterling, Illinois, Matthew and I passed another woman and her son of about sixteen fishing on the bank of the Rock River.

"Did you catch a fish?" Matthew asked them politely.

The woman smiled at him proudly and lifted up a catfish she'd just reeled in.

Still uncomfortable with Matthew's affinity for strangers, I tugged his hand, reminding him of our picnic with waiting relatives. Reluctantly

Matthew turned, dropped his gaze to his feet, and began walking. After a few steps, as if his spirit would not allow him to remain squeezed into a false, speechless straitjacket, he stopped suddenly, lifted his head and called out over his shoulder, "Have a good time fishing, guys."

The fishermen smiled and waved back.

With a renewed spring in his step, Matthew ran off toward the picnic shelter.

As I covered the remaining distance alone, it occurred to me why I as a father, perhaps, teach my children not to talk to strangers. Like the lady at the supermarket, I am guilty of being afraid. The stupid thing is that, honestly, I am not so much afraid of what might happen if I speak to a stranger, but of what they might think of me. Inside, like Matthew, my heart is really crying out for me to reach out to anyone I meet. Unfortunately, too often my head has gotten in the way.

As if I had somehow been made young again, like Tom Hanks returning to his childhood age in the movie *Big*, I turned back toward the fishermen and waved myself. "Good luck."

I'm tired of being afraid.

Dancer of the heart

"Let's leave it here, Big Guy," I said to Matthew early one June morning as I strapped him into his car seat and tugged on the ever-present sword in his hand. In reality it was just a muddy shred of tree bark. Surveying our toy cluttered van, it was obvious we didn't need another artifact to add to our already ample mobile collection.

"No, I'll need it," he mumbled, his eyes half closed with sleep. He clutched the bark tighter and nodded off.

Rather than risk rousing him with further argument, I relented. We had a three-hour drive ahead of us and the last thing I wanted cooped up in the car with me at 6:30 on a Sunday morning was an angry three-year-old. Like an interconnected pair of burglar alarms, set Matthew off and one-year-old Emily was sure to follow. Piercing stereo shrieking louder than most car alarms was not for me that morning, thank you. I didn't want anything to ruin that day.

My brother, Tom, had invited me to an airshow in Oklahoma City. It had been such a long time, ten years maybe, since I'd last seen one. I'm a sucker for airplanes. A couple of days earlier Nel had given me a model airplane in anticipation of Father's Day. It and the airshow had been on my mind for days. Nel and the kids would visit Grandma and Grandpa while Tom and I took in the all-day show.

All the way to Oklahoma City I squinted into the rising sun imagining, Walter Mitty-like, waves of Jap Zeroes diving out of the glare at my lumbering transport plane headed for base in Oklahoma City. We took a couple of hits, but I fought them off in my mind, imagining my van elusively jinking through the skies.

Safely on the drive at Grandma's, I delivered my cargo with a quick "hello" before Tom and I headed off to the airshow.

It was an aluminum dream come true. B-1 bombers. Stealth fighters. The Thunderbirds. Stunt planes by the score. Then came a dazzling flight by Shawn Tucker, a young stunt pilot. As his routine unfolded, I never knew an airplane could do such things. Judging fromthe "oohs" and "ahs" and gasps rising from the crowd, neither did anyone else.

Halfway through his performance, Tucker called in over the loudspeaker for the taped music to be changed. He said he was dedicating the remaining portion of his "sky dance," as he called it, to Tom Jones, a pilot who had been killed during the same airshow the year previous "and, on this Father's Day, to all fathers whose children make their hearts dance." The song? *Love's Theme* by the Love Unlimited Orchaestra.

With the first notes of the music, my heart crashed. An image of my father flashed into my mind. I had forgotten. No present. No card. Not so much as an uttered "Happy Father's Day" to him as he was trimming his lawn when we had arrived.

The realization of my selfishness robbed the rest of the airshow of much of its luster. I was angry with myself. I'd loused up Father's Day.

I wasn't much in the mood to celebrate when we got back to my parents' place late that afternoon. When I opened the door, Matthew raced up to me.

"Happy Father's Day!" he crowed. For the first time in days, his bark sword was missing. In its place was a fancy, hand-made, Matthew-sized wooden sword. "See what Grandpa made me for Father's Day?" he beamed, brandishing the wooden weapon like a junior Errol Flynn.

I mumbled a "Happy Father's Day" in Dad's direction and proceeded to downplay the airshow.

Dad caught me jealously eyeing the new sword. "Since Matthew gave me his, he needed a new one." He turned to Matthew, "We had fun making it, didn't we, Goose?"

"Uh huhhh!" Matthew bubbled, jumping into Grandpa's lap.

It was easy to see from the broad smile on his face, Dad's heart was dancing.

Why can't everything be that easy to see?

A little boy sees a piece of bark as a sword. A grandfather sees that same bark as a gift. That same man sees Father's Day as a time for giving, not receiving.

Real vision. That's what it must take to be a dancer of the heart as accomplished as my father.

Maybe someday, I pray, I won't be so blind.

Seeds of future harvests

"**D**on't go, Papa," Matthew wailed as I pulled on a dusty green and yellow baseball cap. His brown eyes brimmed with tears as they looked up into mine. He wrapped his arms and legs in a death grip around my right calf. "Papa won't come home to me," he sobbed, burying his face in my jeans.

"Sure I will, Matthew," I said, tousling his brown hair and looking to Janel to pry him loose.

She gingerly pulled him away, but it didn't help. His crying got even louder. She sat down at the kitchen table and cradled him on her lap.

"Papa will be back when he's done cutting wheat tonight," Janel said, stroking Matthew's hair.

"No... he... won't," Matthew squeezed out between spasmodic sobs before breaking down once more into tears.

His prediction spooked me. I'd been helping John Scripsick cut his wheat on and off between rainstorms for the last two weeks. I try to be careful around farm machinery, but combines have so many belts, pulleys, and chains whizzing around on them at dizzying speed, all it takes is one mistake. A chill shivered up my spine. I prayed he didn't know something I didn't.

It wouldn't be the first time.

"Listen, listen, Matthew," Janel comforted, rocking him back and forth. "Papa will be safe."

Apparently she was on the same wavelength as I was.

"Yes... but... but... but..." Matthew stammered between sobs and snorts, "...but Grandpa John will love him, and Papa won't come home. He'll go live with John."

The floodgates opened up once more and Matthew buried his face in Janel's shoulder.

Whatever brief consolation I'd taken from his belief that I would be safe melted with his continued tears. Even though they weren't falling on my shoulder, like droplets of invisible acid, they ate through me to the core. I bent down and hugged both Matthew and Janel.

"Matthew, I love you. I'll never leave you," I said.

No sooner were the words out of my mouth than I realized how empty they were. It's a promise a father can only hope to keep.

"John loves Papa and Papa won't come home," Matthew sobbed once more into Janel's shoulder.

She waved me toward the door with her free hand.

It wasn't a very pleasant day in the harvest field for me. I sat in a steamy truck cab between runs to the grain elevator mulling over Matthew's fears when it occurred to me: maybe he wasn't worried so much about my professed love for him. Maybe he was feeling he couldn't love me enough—he felt powerless. After all, he was only three years old.

That realization made me sadder than I had been before. How had Matthew come to feel that? How had he come to feel that he had to compete for my love and, more importantly, that he couldn't win?

It should have been obvious to me all along. To a three-year-old love equals time. Matthew knows I spend more time at work than with him. I spend more time sleeping than with him. Hell, I spend more time on the lawnmower in the average summer week than I do with him. Little wonder then, when I had spent the major portion of the last two weeks cutting wheat with John, that he thought he was losing me to John.

I pulled off my sweat-soaked cap and tossed it on the truck's seat. I combed my hair with my fingers and thought of Matthew and Emily. What's a guy to do? If I don't go to work, they don't eat. The weeds in the yard have to be cut sometime. None of John's kids were able to make it back to the farm to help with harvest that year and he couldn't affort to hire help, so I had offered.

And there I was.

Later that night, dusty and grimy, I stepped into the kids' bedroom to give them kisses. Matthew was sleeping soundly in his bed. Emily stirred in her crib. I hadn't come up with any answers that day, at least I didn't think I had. But the longer I knelt between their beds in the dark as the ceiling fan washed a cool breeze over us, the more one thing did become painfully clear—the seeds of future harvests are being sown right now.

Kiss it all better

I had just zipped my jeans when Matthew, still sleepy eyed, wandered into our bedroom on a Saturday morning. Fully dressed, he stood next to the bed, one hand rubbing his eyes as I bent to pull on my socks. Seeing the ugly scars criss-crossing my left foot, he looked up at me and asked, "Papa got an 'owie?'"

"Yes, Matthew. Papa's got an 'owie,'" thanks to a car wreck that shattered my leg and crushed my foot the year Janel and I married. Until now, apparently, Matthew had never seen my foot. I rarely see it myself except when I'm in the shower.

Matthew bent down and kissed my foot. "It's all better, Papa. Matthew kissed it all better."

I wish.

I let out a sigh and laid back on the bed. Because of my foot I hadn't played a set of tennis in five years. I wasn't that good mind you, but I did enjoy the game. Nor had I been able to run across a field pulling a kite into a cloud-filled summer sky. The longer I lay on the bed thinking of what I hadn't done, the more depressed I became. I hadn't walked barefoot in soft spring grass with the kids. I hadn't squished mud between my toes. It came as little consolation that at least I hadn't felt the pain the doctor warned I might with changes in the weather.

"Come on," Nel called from the kitchen, eager to get on with our monthly shopping excursion. "Let's go. Emily and I are getting in the car."

Once a month, after payday, we drove to Enid, Oklahoma, or Wichita, Kansas, to shop because there was nothing more than a post office and a gas station in the tiny town of Capron, where we lived.

Matthew and I window-shopped on the downtown square in Enid while Nel and Emily picked up a few odds and ends. A light breeze stirred drifts of elm seeds in the doorways of a couple of closed stores. A few shoppers, mostly older folks, made their way in and out of businesses up and down the street. Matthew and I stopped to explore the camera store where we did a lot of looking but no buying. As we strolled down the block toward Woolworth's where we were supposed to meet Nel, I couldn't help but feel that we were caught in a time warp. This is how people spent weekends downtown fifty years ago.

Tugging at my hand, Matthew brought me back

to the future. "Come on, Papa. Let's run," he said.

"I can't run, Matthew."

He rolled his eyes and shot me a stupefied glance. "Yes you can," he said as if I had been pulling his leg.

In the face of such optimism, I didn't want to admit to myself again that I couldn't, that in some fashion I was handicapped. I just walked along holding Matthew back like a strong pier holding a tethered motorboat against the strain of its racing engine.

As we neared the corner he kept pulling. Traffic whizzed past. We live in the country. Matthew's not used to traffic. I gripped his hand tighter, but he broke loose and darted for the curb.

"Matthew!" I screamed as he raced headlong toward the street.

And then it happened, but I didn't realize it until I was standing next to the traffic light at the corner, Matthew cradled safely in my arms. As I lectured him sternly about the dangers of traffic and the need to do what Papa says, I stopped in midsentence.

I had run.

We crossed the street and I set Matthew back on the sidewalk. Now it was my turn. "Come on, Matthew. Let's run."

He smiled and took off again with me in tow. I was limping a bit, but, make no mistake about it, I was running. We raced right past Woolworth's door and on down the block. We turned and ran back, laughing giddily.

I was a little winded when we found Nel, but from the look on her face, I didn't have to say a word. She had seen it all through the window.

I haven't played tennis since then, but Matthew and Emily and I have run through the wheatfield and have flown kites together.

Deep inside I always knew that mothers' kisses held a special healing power. Now I know that little boys' kisses do too.

I'm not a wise man anymore

As I made my way home from a course I was taking at the University of Central Oklahoma late one night, my brain continued to roil with the grisly details of a recent sex crime and the replay of what I thought had been a wise and reasoned argument earlier in the day with one of my own journalism students. The churning thoughts had made it almost impossible to concentrate in class. After reading about the crime in the morning newspaper, I had not been of a mind to listen very closely to my professor's discussion of the sexual symbolism in Chaucer's *Canterbury Tales*. Halfway into my 154-mile drive home, I pulled off the two-lane highway to phone my wife.

I stood at the pay phone in front of the small town's closed convenience store waiting for the call to be connected. Dry leaves skittered eerily across the pavement into the overgrown weeds and brush in the vacant lot next door. A chill snaked its way up my spine. Mingled with the breeze, I could swear I heard the moans and whimpers of the boy sadistically tortured, beaten and left to die amid the weeds of a drainaged ditch in Norman, Oklahoma.

Tired after having worked a full day, driven three hours, sat in class for another two hours, and now having driven an hour and a half toward home, something inside my head seemed to snap. My mind careened out of control, painting the image generated by the story in the newspaper of a small boy, battered and bruised, lying naked on the ground, drenched in blood. The face was swollen and bloodied, the left eye pried from its socket.

Choking for breath, a wave of prevomit nausea swept over me just as Nel's voice came on the line.

"Are the kids OK?" I found myself asking stupidly before I even said hello.

"Fine—" Nel said with a pause, obviously bewildered. "Are you OK?"

"I'm... I'm just tired," I said, swallowing hard and catching my breath. "I just needed to hear your voice."

Back on the road a moment later, I tried to soothe my mind by cranking the tape player volume as high as it would go. It helped until the lyrics from *Carry on Wayward Son* by the group

Kansas stung me with guilt in stereo—if one claims to be a wise man, it surely means he is anything but.

The song tossed me smack into the middle of the argument about pornography and freedom of the press I'd had with one of my older students earlier in the day. "Look, I know what I'm talking about," I had said to him bluntly. "I've studied the Constitution. We can't chip away at the First Amendment just to attack pornography," I argued. "You just don't understand do you, Alan?" I asked derisively.

Alan studied the changing leaves on the trees outside my office window for a long moment before asking calmly, "Did the little boy in Norman understand?" He continued to look out the window. "Did you know that this month's issue of *Hustler* magazine ran an article describing a similar incident of sexual torture? Did you know it hit the newsstands the morning the Norman boy was mutilated?"

I could feel the blood draining from my face—he'd trumped me.

He then proceeded to argue that a civilized legal system must hold pornographers responsible for actions stemming from their words.

Undaunted, I scoffed, "How can you believe that?" in an attempt to end the debate, my voice rising.

Alan slowly picked up his books from the chair across from my desk. "Because," he said, glaring at me intently, "idealism just doesn't cut it, pal." With that, he turned sharply and walked from my office.

As I dragged into my bedroom late that night it struck me how he, the father of two teenage children himself, could believe what he did. It was right before my own eyes. One-year-old Emily lay sleeping in Nel's arms. Three-year-old Matthew was curled by her side, his "blankie" enfolded firmly in his grip. Instead of carrying them to their beds, I stood there watching them sleep peacefully, saddened that the world has grown to be such a dangerous place.

Changing my clothes by moonlight, I couldn't escape the burden of protectiveness I felt. I knew in my heart that Alan had been right. Idealism wouldn't keep my family safe. And, although he hadn't said it, one other thing was true: Matthew's and Emily's papa is a hypocrite.

Despite my respect for freedom of expression, as the crime in Norman came to mind once again, I couldn't shake the rising primal instinct I felt that if I discovered someone sadistically molesting my children, I'd kill him. I would. And in my passion I would probably kill the scum who put the ideas in his head in the first place—First Amendment be damned at my own hand.

I'm not a wise man anymore.

Things that go bump in the night

Something was definitely amiss when I woke up from a sound sleep one spring night. I was spooked. I sat up in bed, peered into the darkness, and craned my neck, listening intently.

Nothing.

No thunder. No dogs barking. No odd sounds from the leaky toilet in our bathroom. Janel slept silently beside me.

I settled back onto the pillow and listened a while longer. The loudest sound was the hurried rush of blood pumping through the veins in my ears.

I'm not a light sleeper. The kids can climb over me to get into our bed in the middle of the night and I won't notice until morning.

There were no kids in our bed this night, even though I'd loved to have found them there to explain away my strange wakefulness.

Something just wasn't right.

The longer I lay there in the stillness the more the

feeling grew that there was definitely something or someone in that house with us.

I looked over the edge of the bed to the blanket on the floor where our brown and white short-haired mutt lay sleeping halfway beteween us and the open bedroom door. Why wasn't she barking? An icy pang gripped me—had this mongrel buddy of mine for the past eleven years died unnoticed right there beside me, her passing spirit rousing me from sleep?

I was afraid to call her name, Mary Ellen, certain she wouldn't stir, only confirming the fact she was no longer there to protect me. The dim light from the waxing moon spilled across her immobile form. Her muzzle lay gently on her paws. I gazed at her for the longest time, recalling the day she and her fuzzball sister had appeared at my doorstep as pups when I lived alone out on the farm during college.

Suddenly, as if the pressure of my gaze had stirred her, Mary Ellen sighed loudly, stretched, and lay over on her side proving she was merely sleeping.

Strangely, I wasn't relieved. The presence I had felt earlier was all the more palpable.

I sat up in bed again and beads of sweat on my brow chilled in the gentle breeze from the ceiling fan. The lighted clock on the dressing table across from the foot of the bed stared at me.

12:04.

Someone or something was definitely playing with

my mind.

Determined to meet my fear head on, I tossed the covers off, got up and walked through the darkened house checking each door and window in turn. After checking the windows in the kids' room, I sat down at the head of Emily's bed, watching her sleep, wondering if her father were losing it.

I'd been working so hard lately. Too hard, probably, for the results I'd gotten. Following a move from the farm back to the city and a new job, I'd spent little time with my children and practically no time with Janel. What had I gained for all my work to stay ahead of the bill collector and climb another rung on the corporate ladder?

Here two-and-a-half year-old Emily slept so peacefully. "Angel Baby" a sitter had nicknamed her. So she was. Her breathing was so gentle. What a counterpoint to my raging anxiety. Each beat of her heart made a tiny ripple in the smooth skin at the base of her neck.

Lazy calculations played through my head. If our hearts beat about sixty times a minute, that's 86,400 times per day, about 31 million beats a year. How fast they slip away. At the average lifespan of sixty-seven years for a male born in 1958 I have—

As if the stranger I feared had just stepped out of the shadows, a shiver ran up my spine—moments ago on that very night, honest to goodness, I'd passed the thirty-three-and-a-half year mark in my life.

I'd crested the hill.

Sitting in the dark stroking Emily's hair, I wondered if I'd used my time wisely.

Sadly, as I replayed the events of my recent past, the answer that came that night was: not often enough.

Just then Mary Ellen wandered in as if to invite me back to bed, my late night odyssey completed.

Had it been some sort of biological alarm or a nudge from God that had roused me from sleep that night to contemplate my life? I'll never know, obviously, but one thing is clear: God willing, Emily, Matthew, Janel, and I have scarcely a trillion beats left to share.

Angry eyes

During one of the rare breaks in the rain on a Saturday afternoon in May, I grabbed the opportunity to take restive Emily and Matthew outside to swing before the rain moved in again. It felt good to be outside. The sun shone brilliantly from between the broken cumulus clouds. The breeze blew light and warm through the slender branches of the young crab apple tree we'd just planted near the swing set. Emily crawled into her swing and giggled with glee as I strapped her in and gave her a big push.

Even though he didn't need my help, Matthew stood in front of his swing, arms outstretched, waiting for me to place him in it.

As I reached down to pick him up he looked into my eyes and a pinched look came over his face, "Papa, why do you have angry eyes?" he asked.

I sucked in a shallow breath, stunned by such a prescient question. "What?" I asked, stalling, as I took stock of the expression I imagined to be on my face.

"You've got angry eyes. Why?"

"Well," I began, searching my mind for some explanation, "it must be because the sun is so bright today. I'm not angry. I'm squinting."

"Oh," he said, unconvinced, as I sat him in his swing and stepped behind to push him and Emily.

I don't know how long we spent outside that afternoon. I lost track of time as I wondered why I appeared angry to my son. No answer had come by the time raindrops began splattering us, chasing us inside.

The answer still had not come by the time my wife and I went to bed later that night. She snuggled close and lay her head on my shoulder. As I softly stroked her auburn hair I was suprised when I thought I felt a tear fall from her cheek onto my chest.

I strained in the darkness trying to see if she were actually crying or if it were just my imagination. Before long Janel's one tear turned into two, and two turned into three, and then there was no turning back. It was a little frightening; Janel is rarely given to tears.

"I miss Annah dog so much," she sobbed softly into my neck.

The words "Me, too," caught in my throat as

memories of our five-year-old Doberman pinscher, whose body we'd buried the week before beneath the crab apple sappling in our backyard, came rushing back. She'd died after Janel had struggled for more than three months to save her life following surgery for an intestinal obstruction.

Janel raised her head from my shoulder to look in my own eyes that were now running with tears. "It hurts so bad," she said and laid her head back on my chest. Her hand gripped my shoulder tightly.

Through the tears, a Sunday morning nearly six years before came back to mind. Janel, then my fiancee, had strolled into my hospital room with an impish grin on her face. I was in the hospital recuperating from a nearly fatal car wreck. She had closed the door behind her and walked over and laid a beige handbag on my bed. Before she could open it a little black nose poked out, soon followed by the unmistakeable black and tan muzzle of a Doberman puppy. Words didn't come then either, just tears of joy as the puppy clawed its way up my chest and, between snorts of pungent puppy breath, began licking my chin.

This puppy, that we immediately named Annah, was a replacement for Kasha Annah, Janel's first Doberman that had been with me in the car the night of the wreck. Untended in an animal shelter, she had died the next day of internal injuries.

Having nursed Kasha back to health from a nasty viral infection as a puppy, I know Janel had been especially hurt at her death, too, even though she'd never told me.

Janel and I cried enough tears for Kasha and for Annah both that night in May.

Sometime after Janel had fallen asleep with her head on my chest, I came to understand that Matthew had been right. I did indeed have angry eyes. I had been angry with God that he hadn't breathed life back into Kasha and that he had done nothing to prevent Annah from dying. And, as I rolled over that night, I couldn't help but wonder how many times I'd failed as a father to breathe life into the things that mean so much to my family.

The priceless gift of life

Annah spent her last evening with me in much the same way as we had spent our first day together. This time, though, the roles were reversed.

An IV tube snaked from a bag overhead, but it dripped fluid into her veins, not mine. I scratched her gently behind the ears as she lay on a blanket spread on our living room floor. It didn't seem like five years had passed since the Sunday my wife had carried her as a puppy with a green nylon collar into the hospital room to meet me.

Annah raised her head and licked my hand and looked me in the eye.

It brought back memories of morning—no one morning in particular, but every morning. At the first sound of someone stirring in our room, she would saunter in and sit patiently at our bedside. Her little stub of a tail would wag furiously, and then, as if she could contain her happiness no longer, she would break out with a smile.

Honest.

As Annah and I sat in the living room that last night, I longed for one last smile, but as I watched the fire in her eyes grow ever dimmer, I knew it would never come.

I'd overheard Janel's phone conversation with the vet a few minutes before. It was time. Annah had suffered enough.

Protectively, I didn't want to let go of this companion who had welcomed me back to life after I nearly died. Somehow I felt if I just hung on a few minutes longer, prayed just a little harder, she'd be cured.

"Give Annah dog a kiss," Janel told Matthew and Emily as she sat down next to us on the floor and clipped a leash to Annah's collar.

"Why are you crying, Mama?" Matthew asked.

Janel took him into her lap and Emily crawled in too.

"You know Annah's been very sick," Janel began, wiping the tears from her face.

"She'll get better," Matthew said confidently, nodding his head optimistically.

"No, Matthew," Janel's voice cracked, "Annah won't get better. She's going to go live with God now."

"Why? She can stay with us."

Janel dabbed at the mascara that ran in streams down her face and looked in my direction for help.

I was no help; I couldn't talk either.

After a long pause she finally whispered, "Kiss her goodbye, guys."

Thirty minutes later Janel returned from the vet's office. Sitting on the tailgate of our minivan next to Annah's body, Janel patiently explained the mysteries of the circle of life and death to Matthew and Emily.

I couldn't bring myself to listen. With darkness approaching, I busied myself digging a grave. All I knew was that Annah was dead, God hadn't spared her life, and I was angry.

We buried Annah at twilight.

In the months that followed, Janel looked carefully for a new puppy. She scoured the papers. She made scores of phone calls. She spent evenings at dog shows. But, mostly, she prayed.

Me? I said I didn't care. If we found a dog, fine. If we didn't, fine. All I knew was it wouldn't be Annah.

When Janel called me one afternoon and told me she and the kids had picked up a puppy, I found something strange happening. With each passing moment I was growing giddy with expectation. Unable to contain myself, I finally snuck away from work and drove home.

Janel and I watched from the back door as the little Doberman puppy wearing the green nylon hand-me-down collar chased Matthew and Emily around the yard. The shrieks of their joyful laughter filtered in through the glass.

Janel put her arm around my waist. "Well? What do you think?" she asked.

The sight of the kids and the puppy playing in the tall grass touched me beyond words. It took a couple of tries before I could give voice to my thoughts. "Have you given her a name yet?"

"How does 'Lakaya' sound."

I looked at her, puzzled.

"You know, *Fiddler on the Roof*. 'To life! To life! Lakaya!'" she sang, parodying one of the show's songs. "Get it? Like the word *l'chaim* only prettier and easier to spell."

I did get it. Whatever vestiges of anger I had been harboring over Annah's death vanished in a flash.

In that special way of hers, Janel had once again brought to me the priceless gift of life.

Land the plane now

"Wow, Papa!" Are you going to fly this plane," bright-eyed, four-year-old Matthew asked excitedly, his nose pressed to the glass at Will Rogers World Airport. The sight of the ground crew scurrying to ready the gleaming yellow and red 737 on the ramp held our four-member family transfixed.

I wish.

"No, but I am going to fly *in* it," I said, giving his hand a squeeze.

"Oh," he said, the tone of his voice betraying his disappointment.

Janel reached out to take two-year-old Emily from her perch on my arm. "Come on, Em. Papa's got to go."

"Go, too!" Emily squealed, hugging my neck tighter.

Go instead, I thought.

The attendant at the Southwest Airlines gate stood impatiently slapping a stack of already-collected

plastic boarding passes against his palm, waiting for
mine, the last one, to complete his collection.

"Emily, come on. Papa's in a hurry," Janel said.

No, I really wasn't. No sane person relishes hur-
tling headlong at 500 m.p.h. toward an angry con-
frontation with an auto mechanic who is holding his
van hostage hundreds of miles from home.

I wouldn't be making this trip had our van's
transmission not shelled out north of Kansas City
while we were returning from vacation two weeks
before. And, yes, I thought, the repair shop had stuck
it to me.

Janel wrestled Emily from my arm as the gate
attendant took the pass from my hand.

"Bye, Papa," Emily waved. "Love you."

I felt so out of control as I stepped onto the crowded
plane. I ended up in the aisle seat of the very last row.
While the plane taxiied for takeoff the stewardesses
went through their obligatory safety song and dance.
It was of some comfort to recall that in the majority of
airline crashes, the tail section often survives intact.

I hoped some section of me would remain intact
following my run-in with the mechanic.

Oh, well. I was here. I was locked in, strapped down
and there was no turning back. We were accelerating
down the runway and the wheels soon broke ground
as we rapidly climbed toward 23,000 feet.

Farm fields zipped by below. I couldn't help but

think of the "NOVA" episode on the hypersonic National Space Plane currently under development. Sometime in the first decade of the next century we'll be able to travel non-stop from New York City to Tokyo in less than two hours.

It boggles the mind. In only a hundred years to have gone from horses and buggies capable of traveling a couple of dozen miles in a day, to automobiles, to space planes traveling ten thousand miles in under two hours. What progress! It felt good to think that I'm part of it.

A stewardess walking the aisle handed me a couple of packets of airline brand fear-suppresant peanuts. I began to tear one open when a hazy image of Matthew and Emily crossed my mind.

"Papa, what did you bring us?" the vision of Matthew asked.

In my mind I was instantly transformed into a child again, my own arms encircling my father's knees, the same words having come from my mouth as he set his luggage on the floor following one of his occasional business trips.

"Me," the memory of my father always said with a big grin.

"Oh," I remembered saying dejectedly.

I don't recall the expression on my father's face at those times, but as a father myself, I could now imagine the depths of his disappointment. Still, he never failed to retrieve some memento of his trip for each of us from some nether corner of his suitcase.

I crammed the peanut packets into my shirt pocket for my own kids and shut my eyes, fighting the tears of shame welling in them, resolving to thank my mother and father for the unselfish gift of themselves over the years to me and my brothers and sister.

A few minutes later one of the stewardesses' voices came over the P.A., "Please dispose of all debris accumulated on the flight at this time—papers, cups, glasses, cans, books, spouses, small children..."

I know she had only meant to be reassuring and humorous as the plane prepared to land, but I was not amused. Fears of my impending meeting had faded, having been replaced with the conviction that maybe, as a husband and father, I'm not too far gone yet. If the price for remaining up to speed with the jet age is to consider my spouse and children accumulated debris, land the plane now, it's time to get off.

We'll make it somehow

"So, if I don't get a second job, just where in the heck do you expect me to get the money?" I whined to Janel, tossing our monthly stack of bills on the kitchen table.

"Just simmer down," she said looking at me sternly. Her glare softened as I pulled off my tie and sat down to dinner. "We're in this together. Remember?"

I grumbled something and picked up the $1,700 car repair bill. "Why didn't we trade in this car before the transmission went out?"

"Because we didn't have the money," Janel replied.

Her answer to my question which hadn't needed one set me off again. "Well we sure as hell didn't have the money to pay for a new transmisson!"

"Look," Janel said, putting a hand on my arm, "I didn't make that transmission go out. You didn't make it go out and neither did these two kids. So, just give it a rest. Please."

Matthew weighed in with a four-year-old's opinion,

"Papa, don't be angry with Mama."

I shot back in a gruff tone, "I'm not angry with Mama—"

Janel squeezed my wrist, stopping me in midsentence. Inside I knew they were both right, but that knowledge just compounded my torment. I wanted to yell and scream and gripe. Life wasn't fair and I wanted someone to know about it.

As if she had calculated how to stem the anger flowing from within me, two-year-old Emily piped up from across the table, "Papa, guess what?"

I knew what was coming, but I wanted to wallow in my discontent a while longer so I didn't answer.

"Papa! Guess what?" Emily insisted more loudly.

"What?" I finally mumbled.

"I love you," she said sweetly, a broad grin accentuating her dimples.

"I love you, too, Em," I answered, the tone of my voice softer now.

Janel let go of my wrist.

We ate our bacon, lettuce, and backyard-garden-fresh tomato sandwiches in relative tranquility, our dinner conversation turning to less stressful matters. We even had a laugh or two before Emily and Matthew finished and rushed off to play.

Janel collected up the leftovers and began making one last sandwich, asking if I'd share it with her.

"Sure," I said, sitting back, mystified by her odd

culinary gyrations. She had put the top piece of bread on the sandwich, raised her knife to cut it, but stopped and rotated the top bread half a turn before finishing, handing me half.

"Why did you turn that piece of bread just now."

"This way we each get some of the sesame seeds. I thought you'd like some, too."

Our conversation turned back to money matters. We could get a loan to cover the car repairs, but it would stretch our single-income budget to the limit. Our discussion trailed off and I got up to return to the office to finish some unfinished business.

Janel kissed me goodbye. "It's been nice staying home with the kids," she said, stepping out onto the porch and shutting the door behind us, "but I guess it's time for me to go back to work."

I was glad she'd suggested it instead of me. I had thought about it from time to time, but was afraid to broach the subject because I knew she took the vocation of being a full-time mom so seriously.

"I guess we could send the kids to the daycare place around the corner," she added, closing the car door after I had climbed inside.

I was still thinking about what she said when I flopped onto our bed later that evening while she read stories to the kids in their room across the hall. The ceiling fan swirled overhead stirring the warm air. The air conditioner was on, but we had set it at eighty-five to save money. I relished the thought of being able to turn it down in the near future.

Just then Matthew appeared next to my bed holding out his favorite stuffed animal. "Here, Papa," he said giving me his red and yellow dragon, "you can sleep with him and play with him. You can." He touched my forehead and said, "Peace be with you," before toddling back to his own bed.

Later, I held Janel in my arms as she drifted toward sleep, replaying in my mind the simple acts of kindness and love shown me that evening by her, Emily, and Matthew.

God knows I didn't deserve them. And he also knows Matthew and Emily didn't learn such selfless generosity from me.

In the dark, I mulled things over for a long time. Would the kids be better off separated from their mother each day? Would our family be stronger? Would the world be a better place?

Recalling the stack of bills on our table and the power saw I'd been itching to buy myself for months, I knew what I wanted the answers to be. But, eyeing Matthew's dinosaur on the pillow next to me, I found myself kissing my wife softly and whispering, "Don't get a job, Nel. We'll make it somehow."

Gold medal all the way

As quietly as I could, I opened the paper one summer Sunday morning, savoring the thought that I might have the chance, for once, to leisurely pore over the pages of virgin newsprint without four-year-old Matthew's or two-year-old Emily's help.

It was not to be. Just as I found the editorial page—my favorite—a short form clad only in a disposable diaper, one hand dragging a blanket behind her, appeared at the arm of my chair.

"Papa, cartoons," she said, crawling up under the newspaper and onto my lap. "Please?"

What's a guy to do? I gingerly folded the editorials, set them down and reached for the comics.

Emily didn't wait for me to open them, she just tore right in, literally, sending ads and the TV guide with Olympic athletes on the cover sliding into a heap on the floor.

"Read, Papa! Read!" she demanded.

For a moment I was lost in the cover of that TV guide. A sense of *deja vu* pulled memories of the winter Olympics back in February to mind.

Despite my general ambivalence toward sports I had watched quite a bit of the winter games. I suppose it was because I had dreamed of turning in an Olympic performance once, after the 1976 games (the Dorothy Hamill games to this then-high school junior). I'd dreamed of a gold medal in cross-country skiing. In a green warm-up suit with yellow and white stripes I began huffing and puffing around our neighborhood at six in the morning. Training lasted for about three days until I drifted into other teenage pursuits like sleeping.

Watching the Olympics in February took the edge off the boring sameness that seemed to have settled over my adult life. The coverage temporarily salved my longings for adventure, my desires to be recognized best in the world at something, anything.

Night after night I imagined cutting graceful figures on the ice with a nimble ice-dancing partner. If nothing else I would have towered head and shoulders above the competition, literally, as the tallest skater at six-foot-seven.

Breathtaking video from cameras mounted on the noses of bobsleds sucked me down the runs along with the teams. Surely, if I hadn't broken off training years ago, with my long legs I could have out-hoofed the fastest pushers.

The more Olympics I watched one night in particular, though, the more difficult it became to escape a smothering feeling that my time for gold had passed.

I had tried to paper over my feelings of inadequacy the next day by putting the kids first, proclaiming it Family Day. After church we went out to eat at their favorite pizza place and topped it off with a visit to the local science museum. It worked pretty well—for a while. We were lost in the learning and the laughter and the fun. It was all we could do to peel Matthew away from the Van de Graff generator that stood his hair on end. I don't know who had more fun, the kids or me. At any rate, the security guard had to practically throw us all out at closing time. What a great day.

Back at home the kids trundled off toward bed and I headed for the tube to catch the last snippets of the Olympic closing ceremonies. As the national anthem played and a montage of athletes with gold medals filled the screen, nagging thoughts that I would never feel a gold medal at my neck swept back in.

Before I could get up to turn the TV off, Emily drifted in dressed in pajamas and crawled into the recliner with me. "Rock, please" she asked sweetly.

I did so, slowly, struck by the realization that my Olympic dreams had been like so many of my other dreams—mere illusions with no real commitment.

Saddened, I wondered if I had the perseverance to accomplish anything important in life.

As if in answer to my unspoken question, Emily snuggled in closer under my arm and three words escaped her lips as she fell asleep, "I'm happy. Happy…"

My eyes watered instantly. All at once I was caught up in the anthem playing from the TV. It wasn't for the athletes parading across the screen, it was for me. My dreams had come true in the little girl cuddled beside me.

In some mysterious way that night, Emily's warmth and words whispered to me, "Gold medal performance, Papa. Gold medal all the way."

What's it going to hurt?

A four-year-old's curiosity over what exactly constitutes fly guts and a discussion of why it isn't polite to play with flyswatters at the dinner table had pretty much ended the meal for my wife and me the other night even though there was food left on our plates. I cleared the table and went to the living room to read, leaving Matthew to chase wildly around the house with his flyswatter in search of empirical evidence on his own.

It didn't take long for me to become engrossed in Jim Lehrer's novel about a one-eyed young Kansan in search of himself in 1950s Oklahoma. Transported back to the days of motorcoach lines, trains, and Grapette sodas, I quickly lost track of all that was happening in my own living room. Only when a little hand shook my book some time later did I emerge in the present.

"Look, Papa, a butterfly!" Emily bubbled.

"Huh?" I grunted, squinting through the plate

glass window at the sky that had since turned dark.

"No, Papa. Look!" Emily said, pointing excitedly at the ceiling.

A tiny flutter of beige flickered in and out of the slowly turning blades of the ceiling fan. On the couch below, Matthew and Janel sat reading that day's catch of library books, oblivious of the moth over-head.

"It's just a moth, Em," I said, turning back to my book.

"Butterfly," she corrected.

It certainly hadn't been a butterfly that had done the damage I'd discovered in my closet a couple of days before when the weather had unexpectedly turned cool. Something had chewed two neat holes through one of my favorite sweaters.

Emily had climbed onto the couch, stepped over Matthew, and was now standing squarely in Janel's lap watching the moth as it bounced around inside the shade of the lamp on the end table.

I eyed the flyswatter laying next to the lamp where Matthew had left it, and began wondering what exactly constitutes moth guts. Just as I set down my book to make a move for the swatter, as if she had read my mind, Emily said, "Papa, the butterfly wants me to catch him."

"Em, he's a moth," I whined. "He eats clothes."

Growing tired of our entemological classification

debate, not to mention the thirty-odd pounds of two-year-old standing in her lap, Nel piped up, "Whatever it is, Jim, would you please catch it for her."

"But—"

"Please!" she said in a tone that was more command than polite request. Her expression softened. "What's it going to hurt?"

Her question immediately brought to mind a long-forgotten question posed by a new acquaintance, Michael Brown, when a group of us had been helping a mutual friend move into a house twelve years before.

Michael had discovered a large spider hiding in a corner and had carefully scooped it into a jar and was taking it outside.

"Why don't you just squash it and be done with it?" I asked.

"What's it going to hurt?" he had asked, walking out the front door.

The rest of us had laughed and, with limp-wristed gestures, questioned Michael's masculinity. It hadn't been until some months later that we learned that Michael had survived several open-heart surgeries as a child but was still living on borrowed time. His gratitude for all life blossomed from deep roots.

As I peered over the lampshade that night, I found myself sharing Michael's respect for life, wanting to catch Emily's tiny butterfly and release it outside. It was kind of pretty. Its wings were light beige with a muted red stripe crossing them horizontally. I cupped my hand and caught it easily.

"Let's put it outside, Em."

"No, let me hold him!"

I really didn't want to, knowing she would probably crush him. I had been so careful to capture him intact. Emily followed me outside where I acquiesced a little by holding my hands close to her before opening them.

Rather than flying off as I would have expected, though, the moth lit on Emily's thumb. She studied him carefully and then waved him toward the sky.

"Goodnight, butterfly. Fly to your family," she called as he flew away.

I swept Emily into my arms, touched by her gentleness and warmed by thoughts of Michael Brown wherever he is, if he still is.

"Come on, Butterfly," I said to Em. "Let's fly inside to our family."

I've been down that road

Gasoline fumes had never given me a problem, so I doubt that's what began clearing my thoughts as I filled the company car's gas tank at a convenience store one spring Tuesday morning. I don't think the Oklahoma breeze that kept flipping my tie up over my shoulder did it either. I don't even think it was the long stare of the attendant drilling through me when I handed her my credit card.

But, as I peeled the wrapper from a Hershey bar and eased the blue Grand Am onto the highway leading away from Shawnee a couple of minutes later, the mental facade I'd erected around a hastily prepared business trip was definitely cracking. With the first haunting sounds of swirling wind and the driving drumbeats of Christopher Cross's *Ride Like the Wind* blaring from the stereo, the illusion came crumbling down—I wasn't on a business trip at all.

I was running away.

Less than ten minutes before, my secretary had looked a little surprised when I asked her for the keys to the company car.

"Oh, yeah, I had this trip planned for some time," I told her.

Yeah, all of fifteen minutes—the time it had taken for the idea of the trip to hatch after having caught a trusted co-worker in a lie.

Maybe it shouldn't have bothered me. Maybe it was none of my business. But whenever a colleague preaches to me the virtues of openness and honesty one moment and then in the next moment I discover that he was hiding a botched performance on his part from his boss by pressuring a friend of mine, I call that a lie.

I set the cruise control, loosened my "power" tie and unbuttoned the collar of my starched shirt.

Oh, sure, I had assembled packets of marketing literature to leave with contacts along the way as my 194-mile trip into the approaching rural Oklahoma afternoon unfolded. As the public relations director, after all, it was my job to keep key publics informed, I reasoned. And, yes, I would be speaking with a valued public relations colleague of mine at the terminus of my trip.

Am I living a lie? I began to wonder.

No, I reassured myself, I just didn't want to be in the office. I didn't want to be around two-faced people.

Even with the stereo as loud as it would go, a little voice sounded clearly in my head as if he had been sitting in the back seat, "Papa, do you sometimes lose your way?" My four-year-old had asked that very question the previous evening as he and I returned home from a grocery run via a circuitous route.

"Sometimes, Matthew," I had answered, not quite sure why.

"That's OK," he had said. "You'll find the way."

With the nose of the company car pointed away from Shawnee, away from my job, away from Matthew, Emily, and Janel, I wasn't so sure.

The rest of the drive and my meeting in Alva was lost in a blur. I didn't even eat lunch. It wasn't until early in the evening when I stepped into the living room of my surrogate parents' house near our previous home on a farm outside of Alva that my heart and mind switched off of automatic pilot.

John took me outside to proudly show off his ripening wheat crop. The setting sun deepened its golden color. Evaporating rainwater from the previous night's thunderstorm carried with it the sweet smell of the wheat.

Over dinner John and his wife listened to my story of disillusionment. By the time dinner was over, my load had lightened and I headed for the door. I felt a profound need to get back to Shawnee to see

Matthew and Emily before they went to bed. Lottie
hugged me and said, "Anytime you need to talk, you
know where home is."

I hugged her tighter.

Yes, I had delivered my literature that day. Yes, I
had a productive meeting with my colleague. I even
conducted an impromptu desktop publishing semi-
nar at the college in Alva.

But, honestly, at it's heart, the trip was not about
business. It was about wheatfields, sunsets and
hugs from people I miss. It was about finding truth
when I thought none existed. It was about going
home.

So, sometime in the future when Matthew or Emily,
or both, feel the need to run away, I pray I'll be a little
slow to judge and more apt to listen and understand.
Because now, even at this late stage, I've been down
that road myself.

I want to be in your picture, Em

It had been one of those grueling days at the office. You know the ones—even though you go in early and stay late, for every job that gets finished two new ones take its place.

So, when I settled into my easy chair before dinner that evening to watch the news with Tom, Peter, Dan, Robin, Jim, Bob, Linda, Jack, Jennifer, Roger, and Jennifer (how woefully uninformed man must have been before the advent of remote control), I wasn't in much of a mood to be disturbed. And, as sometimes happens on days like this one, before I knew it, I was watching the news with my eyes closed.

I don't know how long I had been in that state when I felt something insistently tugging at my channel-changing finger.

"What the—" I growled, my hand groping reflexively for the remote control even before my eyes had opened fully and apprehended the cause for my arousal.

There, standing beside my chair, looking at me with her most innocent look, was two-year-old, Emily. "Papa, swing me," she implored plaintively.

"Emily!" I snapped back, still not quite awake.

Her eyes grew sadder, and more needy. "Please, Papa. Swing me."

Just then Janel's voice piped up from the kitchen, "Let Papa rest, Emily. He's had a hard day."

Emily's lower lip slid slowly forward, the corners of her mouth turning down. Tears welled in her eyes. "Papa won't swing me," she wailed, walking into the kitchen.

Too guilty to continue watching the news yet still too lazy to get up and swing this little girl whom I'd not seen all day, I began flipping through the channels. For some reason an advertisement caught my eye. A man about my age was whirling his young son playfully in the air. The boy's laughter filled the air. Suddenly the scene froze and the screen turned from color to black and white. The laughter faded eerily.

I don't know how the commercial ended because another black and white image had suddenly filled my mind. It was the memory of an old photograph in one of my mom's and dad's photo albums. It was probably one Mom had intended to throw away. It was loose, not pasted in with the little adhesive corners.

In it my smiling brother, Tom, sat on the swing set

in our backyard as a boy of perhaps five. His right index finger was raised dutifully skyward so Mom could focus carefully with her Argus rangefinder camera. The eery thing about that photograph was that it was a double exposure. Somehow Mom hadn't advanced the film, and a wispy, ghostly image of Dad with his toothy, young-adult grin, stood behind Tom. Hauntingly, they weren't part of the same picture.

That picture spooked me the first time I ran across it, and, on this evening, its memory was spooking me again. It spooked me through dinner and through washing dishes.

When I was done, I fought the urge to return to my recliner. I went instead and found Emily playing by herself on the rocking horse in the play room.

"Let's go swing, Em."

I didn't have to say it twice. She sprung into my arms and we went outside where we swang, rather she swang, I pushed. She laughed gleefully as her hair tossed in the breeze. Back and forth, back and forth.

All the while, in my mind, back and forth, back and forth, she swung from a little girl of two to a young woman of eighteen. Her hair much longer, her features soft and mature, I imagined myself still swinging her, talking about boys, and dates, and fears, and dreams, and life.

I found my heart aching to be able to have that kind

of relationship with her sixteen years into the future.

It was well after dark when Janel called us in. Neither one of us wanted to come, but we finally did.

A little later, while I was undressing for bed, I heard the patio door roll open on its track. I looked out the window to see Emily, clad in nothing more than a diaper clambering into her swing.

"Papa, come swing me," she called into the night.

Even in my skivvies, I wanted to go and swing her for as long as she wanted because deep inside I know, despite how preoccupied with other things I might be, if I don't swing her now, there's little chance I'll be in her picture when she's eighteen.

Home is where the neighbors are

My boss's question as the waitress cleared away our lunch dishes one day came at me like a batter's line drive sizzling toward a pitcher on the mound: "Well, it's been a year since you took this job, any regrets?"

My immediate gut instinct was to say no, I was looking for a long future, but for some reason those words didn't come out.

"Sometimes," I heard myself say, "sometimes I honestly wonder if I didn't make a mistake."

The boss's brow furrowed perceptibly above the frames of his glasses.

"The job's fine," I added hastily. "There are times, though, when I don't feel at home here. I've been really homesick lately."

Closer in age to my father than to me, the boss nodded knowingly and turned his water glass round and round with his fingertips where it rested on the table. "I know what you mean. Sometimes I miss

home too. New York is so beautiful this time of year.
The trees. The lakes..."

Wisely, perhaps sensing an impending slip over the
edge into melancholy, he suggested it was time we got
back to work.

Even though our conversation had ended, my
homesickness did not. Throughout the rest of the
day, images of our previous home kept creeping in.
More than our white, one-story farmhouse that stood
in the middle of a wheatfield, I missed John, and
John, and John, Lottie, Terry, Glenn, Georgianna,
Daryl, Liz, Roger, Fred, Don at the gas station who
always gave Matthew and Emily Tootsie Pops, and
the Coxes who ran the Chief Theatre at a loss just so
the kids would have some place to go and something
to do. They all gave so freely of themselves. It was
these people who had taken this city boy and baptized
him into the closeness of life in a small town.

Deep inside, I longed to be born again.

After dinner that night, as Janel was leaving to go
ride horses at the college, I confided that moving had
indeed been a mistake. I felt we didn't belong here.
I was ready to move back. "What do you think?" I
asked her.

She kissed me on her way out the door and said, "If
that's what God needs us to do, he'll let us know."

While the kids watched the *Jungle Book* on video,
I tried to formulate a plan on how we could make the

return. I was pretty sure the farmhouse we had rented was still vacant. As far as work goes, I wasn't sure I wanted to return to the college in Alva. Besides, they may not have wanted me back. I cooked up a couple of ideas for possible businesses, maybe a cheap taco place or a quick oil change franchise.

About that time the phone rang. Of all people, in all honesty, it was one of our neighbors from the farm. An expectant tingle ran up my spine.

"Hey, Jimmy, how's Shawnee treating you?"

"Fine," I lied, making small talk.

"Just thought I'd call to tell you that they burned your old house down the other day. They did. Gave me chills watching it."

Made me sick hearing about it. The feeling was as final as that I'd felt when I learned my first high school crush, Mary Semtner, was getting married. My schoolboy fantasy of life with her died hard. My dream of life on the farm died harder.

At work the next day, I just went through the motions. I don't recall a thing about the day except for Emily running out to the car when I pulled into the drive that afternoon.

"Papa's home! Papa's home!" she shouted.

I wish.

I changed into my work clothes to go outside and fire up the riding lawnmower. I mowed our little

postage stamp of a lawn and, almost without thinking, mowed the neighbors' lawn too. They have
allergies so bad, I hate to see them out mowing
because I know they'll be paying for it for days.
Besides, it only takes me five minutes—

All at once an odd, unseen presence made itself
known. It was as if John, and John, and John, Lottie,
Glenn, Georgianna, Daryl, Liz, Terry, Fred, Don, and
the Coxes were right there with me—they would have
done the same for their neighbors.

For the first time in over a year, I felt good about
being here in Shawnee, Oklahoma. I could hardly
contain my desire to run inside as ecstatic as Emily
had been earlier and shout, "Nel! Matthew! Emily!
Guess what! Papa *is* home!"

A father's tears

I gently closed the book *Good Night Moon* late one night so as not to disturb the bedtime magic it had apparently wrought. Matthew was sleeping soundly on my left arm. Emily was on my right, her eyelids drooping heavily as she cast adrift on that gently rolling ocean separating wakefulness from sleep.

Ever so softly I whispered, "Do you have a good night kiss for me, Emily?" I was sorry I hadn't asked her earlier. She remembers these things. If I didn't get a kiss from her now, I knew I could expect to see her at my bedside sometime in the night crying that I hadn't kissed her.

Emily smiled and turned her head away coyly. "No," she said dreamily, pulling the blanket up to her chin.

"No? Not even one little one?"

Her right thumb found her mouth and she curled her index finger over the bridge of her nose, "Unh,

unh."

"Do you want to see Papa cry," I teased her, feigning sniffles.

Instantly, as if I'd just told her I'd be leaving her, never to return, Emily turned to look at me, her eyes full of fear.

Her expression ripped right through me. I was sorry I'd teased her. "Papa's not going to cry," I reassured her clumsily, hugging her close. "Papa's not going to cry."

I don't think she believed me. She just stared at me intently, saying nothing, but gamely fighting sleep with more pluck than I would have guessed a two-year-old could muster after having been awake for seventeen-plus hours. Ultimately the battle was lost and she closed her eyes.

I carried Matthew to his bed and instead of continuing on into my room, found myself returning to Emily's bedside. I knelt on the floor and leaned down next to her, stroking her fine brown hair as I pondered what was so frightening about seeing her father cry.

I closed my eyes and a memory of a Saturday afternoon in my parents' home in Oklahoma City over ten years before came to mind.

I had been in my bedroom listening to the stereo when I heard the phone in the kitchen ring. It rang only once. I waited a minute, half expecting to hear someone call my name. When no one did, I wandered toward the kitchen anyway, wondering who was on the phone. A few steps from the doorway I heard the phone being hung up and then I heard a mournful sound like none I'd ever heard before, yet it was chillingly familiar. The sobs of my father's crying were almost more than I could bear.

Without asking, I knew Grammer, his mother, had died.

Choking back sobs of my own, I had peered through the doorway carefully, hoping I wouldn't be seen. There, sitting at the small table in the middle of the room was my father, his face buried in his hands. My mother stood behind him, her arms wrapped securely around his shoulders. His strong upper body shook with each sob.

As if I'd willingly stuck my finger in a light socket, the scene shook me.

I turned and ran to my room, accidentally slamming the door before collapsing on the bed. It wasn't long before my mother was there, her arms wrapped securely around me.

A deep sigh from Emily startled me back to the present. I opened my eyes to look at her, but it was difficult to focus clearly through a veil of tears.

At that moment I knew what had frightened her so.

I know there is something reassuring about a father's strength, but since the day my grandmother died, I have felt a certain closeness to my father that

I hadn't felt before. Until that day I had felt I was just a kid with mixed up emotions, dreams and fears. It was me who had been the one to cry many times in his presence during late-night discussions he and I often had in the den after everyone else was in bed. At those times I remember seeing my father as strong and resourceful and hoped that one day I would be like him too.

On the day I heard him cry it was as if he'd pushed over the pedestal I'd put him on and shown me he was just like me, a flesh-and-blood person who could feel as lost and confused and alone and hurt as I often did. His sobs sounded very much like my own.

It was the day I grew up.

So, perhaps it's not the time to cry with Emily just yet. I now believe she needs me to be strong for a while longer until that day—sometime in the future—when a sprinkling of her father's tears will help her grow.

Unfinished business

"Could you help me finish something?" my wife asked politely one evening as I foraged through the kitchen cabinets for junk food to take with me to a football game.

"I really don't have the time," I said, sheepishly stuffing a handful of Matthew's and Emily's leftover Halloween candy into one of my parka pockets as if I were a kid who'd just been caught with his hand in the cookie jar. I was already late leaving for my weekly newspaper assignment. I covered a local high school game each week to pick up a few extra bucks before Christmas.

Working at the kitchen table, Janel struggled to attach a wire hanger to the back of a large picture frame that lay face down in front of her. No matter how hard she pushed, the screw eyes wouldn't bite into the oak frame.

I looked at the clock then back to Janel. "If I'm late and don't get a seat in the press box," I quipped, pulling an ice pick from the knife drawer and wagging it in her direction, "it's all your fault."

Janel eyed the ice pick with mock wariness. "I'm only doing this for you, you know. But go ahead, I think I can finish it myself now."

I made a couple of pilot holes in the picture frame with the ice pick and started a screw eye in one of the holes to ensure it would work. Just then the phone rang and Janel picked it up.

Saved by the bell—or so I thought. I ducked into the living room, but before I could get out the front door, Matthew's voice caught me.

"Papa, would you come finish a game with Emily and me?"

"I'm really in a hurry, Matthew. Maybe another time."

"You never have time to play anymore," he responded dejectedly, slapping his hand onto the coffee table where he and Emily were playing *Chutes and Ladders.*

I gave them both a kiss and walked out the door.

I did get a seat in the press box that night and I didn't have cold feet to bring home to bed. When I got home around one o'clock, though, it was as if my family had simply disappeared. The lights in the living room and kitchen were still on. The picture frame was missing from the kitchen table, but the *Chutes and Ladders* game was still spread out on the coffee table.

It was kind of eery.

I shut off the lights and went to bed, checking first to see that Matthew and Emily were indeed in their beds. I pulled the covers up under their chins.

It didn't seem like I slept long before the alarm clock roused me, summoning me to the word processor for some early morning work on a novel. As had become my custom since football season and late nights at the newspaper started, I found it easier to turn off the alarm and settle in for more sleep instead.

Only that morning sleep wouldn't return. After about thirty minutes of tossing and turning I arose, showered, dressed and ate quickly.

When I flicked on the light in my spare-bedroom office, there on the wall behind my desk hung the frame Janel had been struggling with the evening before. I stopped, transfixed by the picture it held.

A pang of guilt stabbed into me. Gazing at me lovingly was the lithographed portrait of a good friend of mine, HoHo the clown, a local TV personality and lover of children.

That picture had been in my closet gathering dust since my sister gave it to me for Christmas two years before. I hadn't had the guts to put it up. I was ashamed of the biggest piece of unfinished business it represented in my life.

It reminded me of a lunch HoHo and I had years

before during which I agreed to write his biography. It reminded me of a job I took far away soon thereafter. It reminded me of my new boss's admonition to finish HoHo's book before time got away because he, too, was good friends with this incredibly gentle man.

Sitting there that morning, I was reminded of the time I had indeed let slip away and the death HoHo had perhaps sensed was coming when he had asked me to write his story.

I never got it done.

I fought the urge to pull the picture down and put it back in the closet. Instead, I decided to leave it on the wall to gaze over my shoulder. Since that time it has served as a healing reminder, with which I think HoHo would agree, that time slips away, and that a father's time not spent with his family is the saddest unfinished business of all.

He's my hero

I was almost out the door one morning when Matthew called, "Wait, Papa! Don't go yet," as he jumped off the couch and raced down the hall toward the playroom.

"Matthew, I can't wait. I've got an early meeting," I called after him.

His sleep-mussed, brown-haired head appeared at the doorway, his left hand raised in the universal stop signal. "Just a minute, Papa," he commanded firmly, "I'm looking for something." His head and shoulders popped back out of sight.

I fidgeted with the pages of the report I had awakened early to review. I was supposed to present it at my meeting in just a few minutes. "Matthew," I whined, "I'm late."

The rustling noises emanating from the playroom intensified.

My wife stepped out of the kitchen. "What's the problem?"

"I'm late for a meeting and Matthew's trying to find something. I can't wait."

"Well," she said in her diplomatic voice, "you could help him."

Not exactly what I wanted to hear. With doubts filling my mind about how the marketing report I'd worked on for weeks would be received, and with butterflies multiplying in my stomach about what that reception would portend for my future, the last thing I was worried about was helping my son find some hastily remembered moth-eaten trinket to play with in his perpetually messy playroom.

Just as I reached for the front door handle Matthew returned and jammed something into my pocket.

"What was that?" I asked, reaching into my pocket.

Matthew pulled my hand away.

"Just take it to work with you, Papa."

"I just want to carry it," I said disingenuously, intending to leave whatever it was on the seat of my car before I walked in to work.

"No," Matthew said firmly. "Leave it in your pocket. It's something you need to play with at work."

As my mind wandered on my way to work, I forgot to take the toy out of my pocket.

Halfway through my presentation, it was clear I was winning few friends. I nervously thrust my hands into my pockets as I walked about the conference room. My voice halted for a moment when my hand encountered what felt like a figurine where I had expected to find a handful of change. I cleared my throat as if a tickle had been the cause for my pause. My mind eased a bit as I fingered the toy in my pocket and imagined Matthew sitting in the chair I had occupied right next to the boss. In my imagination he sat swinging his feet, listening attentively, eating cookies from the silver tray in the middle of the conference room table. The image helped lighten my thoughts and I was able to take a new approach in explaining my plan.

I don't recall many specifics about the rest of the presentation except a number of pointed questions, lots of cold stares that were slowly replaced by approving nods, and a round of handshakes when the meeting broke up. I didn't stay around long. I couldn't wait to get back to my office and pull the figurine from my pocket.

I have no idea where Matthew came up with the toy I found in my pocket that morning. I hadn't bought it for him, nor had Janel. But there it was in front of me, one of the characters from the movie *Ghostbusters*.

I left it on my desk for days. Everyone who came into my office gravitated toward it, playing with it, bending it into impossible, pretzel positions. It was good for laughs.

One afternoon a couple of days later a letter arrived from one of my former students with whom I had been corresponding since I left my previous school. I sat down at the computer to begin a reply, but I had to stop when I got to the student's question about who were my heroes.

I didn't have any answers. I'd never thought about it. I had stared at the word processor a long time when I heard footsteps in the hall that sounded like my boss's.

Sure enough. He stuck his head in the doorway and motioned toward the toy on my desk. "Is that your hero?"

The coincidence of his question right as I was contemplating that very thought surprised me. I opened my mouth reflexively intending to say no, but something stopped me. The figurine was replaced in my mind by the image of the four-year-old boy who'd presented a mysterious gift that I had almost been too impatient to receive—a simple gift which had helped me successfully collect my thoughts at a critical moment.

With Matthew firmly in mind as an answer to my former student's question, I nodded to my boss. "Yeah. You bet. He's my hero."

To hell in a handbasket

When I pulled into the driveway one November afternoon, Matthew came bursting through the front door, running toward the car. Heartened by his exhuberant welcome, I reached for the door latch.

"Hi, Big Guy!" I called to him.

Before I could get one leg out the door, he slammed it shut and spoke through the open window.

"Promise you'll walk on the sidewalk Papa," he commanded.

So much for a rousing welcome.

"Walk on the sidewalk so you won't step on the leaves and crunch them into bits," he said matter-of-factly. "We're going to rake them into a pile so Emily and I can jump in them." His stern look eased and his eyes brightened. "OK?"

I looked at the fallen leaves scattered across the lawn. Raked together, there wouldn't be a pile big enough for a rabbit to hide under.

"OK," I said, easing the door open.

"Good, because Mama said we'd rake them up when there's enough for a big pile so we can jump in them. Do you want to jump, too?"

I put my hand on his head as we walked up the sidewalk, contemplating his invitation and, more important to me, the evening news program I'd hurried home to see. At the rate the leaves were falling it would be days before there was a Matthew-size pile under the silver maple in the front yard. For tonight, anyway, I could watch my news program in peace.

Inside, I changed clothes and settled into my easy chair in the living room to watch the news special on the elections. I'd followed a number of state and national races closely and I was afraid there was an ample number of candidates who could lead the nation down the road to hell in a hand basket.

Moments into the program, Matthew stuck his head in the front door. "Come on, Papa."

"There's not enough leaves yet, Matthew. Besides, I'm watching something important. I'll be out later."

As if I'd been kidding him about watching some-thing important, Matthew marched to the TV, turned it off and grabbed my hand. "Let's go watch the leaves fall."

I opened my mouth to scold him, but the innocent look in his eye stopped me. I rose from my chair and let him lead me out the door.

"Here we go," he said, crawling up on the wooden porch swing and patting the seat next to him.

I sat down and silently surveyed the tree whose branches stretch from one side of our yard to the other. If Matthew and I were here to watch the leaves fall, we were going to be here a long time. Most of the leaves still bore a dark green hue.

We slowly rocked back and forth on the creaky old porch swing, the two of us, neither saying a word. My thoughts soon turned to the election special I was missing and the cultivated images and calculated lies candidates had hurled at one another for more than a year. It angered and depressed me that politics is such a gutter-level street fight between people to whom winning is the only thing. Still, I wanted to go back inside.

"Look, Papa! There's one," Matthew said, pointing to a leaf tumbling slowly downward.

I watched it settle lightly on the grass and then noticed a neighbor and her teenage daughter walking arm in arm up the street toward us. They waved as they passed. Beyond them, in a yard down the block, two small children were chasing around, laughing and enjoying the fall weather. A rhythmic thunk, thunk, thunk, bump, clatter, swish, thunk, thunk thunk... drifted toward us from next door. Robert, a college student who lived next door, was out shooting baskets on the drive.

"There's another one, Papa!" Matthew squealed again, watching his treasure grow leaf by leaf. He reached a small hand toward mine and took hold of it. Just to hold.

All at once I was gripped by a solid sense that all was as it should be—the important things were right here, not inside on TV. Somewhere, in the sights and sounds of our neighborhood, I had lost my fear of the elections. I was certain that as long as there are little boys who will hold their fathers' hands, mothers who will take leisurely strolls with their teenagers, and fathers who will take the time to watch leaves fall from trees with their children—regardless of which sleazy politician might be in office—America will not be going to hell in a hand basket.

An apple for the teacher

Obviously, in hindsight, I didn't stand a chance even before the fight erupted. Six against one are pretty long odds in anyone's book.

Still, confident of my debating abilities, I waded into a fray against six of my college students one afternoon self-righteously thinking I could dispatch a couple of them quickly with a flurry of verbal punches, convincing another couple to switch to my side before they suffered the same fate.

How conceited can an instructor be?

I got beat up pretty good.

Later that evening, sitting at the dinner table, my pain had drained into the crevices of my consciousness like rainwater running into cracks in drought-parched earth.

I had left the television on. Usually that's a no-no during meals at our house, but I had wanted to catch details of our troop deployment to Somalia. My back

141

to the screen, I wasn't paying much attention. I was more intent on slathering the slice of leftover Thanksgiving turkey on my plate with honey barbecue sauce. Not a big fan of leftovers, I have to admit it was pretty good. As I was saucing up a second helping, four-year-old Matthew drew my attention to the TV.

"Papa? Why is that boy on TV so skinny?"

I turned, finding an emaciated face staring at us from the screen. The Somali boy was lying on what appeared to be a dirty rag on a concrete floor in some dimly lit building. The skin on his face was drawn tightly into the hollows under his cheekbones, emphasizing his eyes and mouth. He made no attempt to shoo away flies crawling over his face.

Instantly, my eyes brimmed with tears and no words would come out of my mouth to answer Matthew's question.

"He's starving, Matthew," Janel answered quietly in my stead, picking at the food on her plate.

Matthew stared intently at the screen, reeling off question after question. Janel continued to find answers.

"Will he die?"

"I don't know."

"Why isn't he crying?"

"He's too weak."

"Is he hungry?"

"Yes, I'm sure he is."

Matthew paused for a moment and looked at his plate. "Mama," he said quietly, setting his fork down, "that boy can have my dinner."

With that, every shred of appetite left my body. I felt the need to sob openly but, for some reason, I couldn't.

Janel looked toward me, her eyes full of tears. Finally, she said, "Matthew, that boy lives ten thousand miles away."

"So," he replied.

So. I was touched by his innocent courage. If only we'd pointed the direction and handed him his coat, Matthew stood ready to serve.

Later, in the wee hours of the morning, snippets of the debate I'd had earlier in the day with the students in my mass communications class wouldn't let me sleep.

We'd spent fifteen weeks learning how to analyze messages and motives in various media. I'd prided myself on trying to teach them how to think, not what to think.

Tossing and turning, I recalled my weak assertions that television was inherently damaging.

Using statistics and studies from their own recently completed term papers, they built a compelling argument to the contrary.

As a teacher, I had naively made the mistake of thinking that if I gave my students intellectual tools they would use them to build the same conclusions I had.

And, recalling the confirmation of their viewpoint at my own dinner table earlier, I was now ready to concede that they were right, I was wrong—television can indeed be a force for inestimable good.

Wide awake, I got up to write. Before I came back to bed that night I wrote a dozen words, tops. It was the most satisfying writing I'd done in a long time.

I wrote two checks to Feed the Children. One in the name of the students in my mass communications class, one in Matthew's name.

As often happens, if teachers will only admit it, students have an awful lot to teach the teacher.

Natika, Beth, Matt, Laurie, Willy, Alexa, thank you. I'll never forget.

A camcorderless Christmas

O ur church's Christmas pageant had barely begun one evening two weeks before Christmas when a friend behind me tapped me on the shoulder.

"Your kids are adorable! You really should move up closer and take some pictures," he urged excitedly above the din in the gymnasium turned auditorium.

Swelling with pride, I replied over my shoulder, "In a minute," pulling a small instamatic camera from my pocket. I set it on my lap. I didn't want to miss a minute of this.

My heart melted watching Emily in the cow outfit Janel had made for her. She sat quietly on a fragrant bed of cedar boughs in the living nativity. Occasionally she shook her head, tinkling the small cowbell hanging around her neck. Her four-year-old brother towered over her, standing on a chair, as one of the angels making up the heavenly host. He kept adjusting and readjusting his halo as if he were a teenager searching for just the rakish angle sure to catch a cute female angel's eye.

The woman sitting in front of me turned and with an enormous smile asked, "Isn't this great? Your kids are so cute."

I could feel my face flush.

As if she'd just realized I were missing some essential item of clothing, her smile faded and one eyebrow arched. "Hey, where's your camcorder?"

The tone of her question caught me by surprise.

"I... I don't have one," I stammered.

She frowned deeply, broke off the conversation and turned around.

The sound system was so poor I had to concentrate hard to hear the children singing but, sensitized by the woman's question, I couldn't help but self-consciously notice camcorders sprouting from fathers' faces throughout the gym.

I did kind of feel naked.

The program ended all too quickly and, equally as quickly, parents and children disappeared into the cold night despite the lure of refreshments and games.

I was ready to talk and share and reminisce about Christmases past.

I guess everyone else had rushed home to view their videos and reminisce about Christmas present.

The whole Christmas pageant-camcorder thing

stuck with me for days. Why did I feel so out of touch with my electronic generation?

It wasn't until I was hefting a plastic sporkful of mashed potatoes at Kentucky Fried Chicken with a friend a couple of days later that it began to make sense. A memory of a night two days before Christmas years before came rushing back.

Covering my first convenience store robbery as a novice photographer at an Oklahoma City television station, I had taped policemen and paramedics emerging from the store feverishly working on a clerk laying on a gurney. They loaded him into an ambulance and, siren blaring, it raced into the night.

I hustled the videotape back to the station and moments later saw it airing as a news bulletin.

I almost threw up.

Squinting at the black-and-white picture in my camera's eyepiece, I hadn't realized at the time how bloody and graphic and gory was the scene I had recorded. Now here it was in color on TV.

Finishing lunch with my friend the other day, it hit me that it wasn't the blood and guts that had sickened me so much as it was the thought that I could be present for something so frought with emotion and yet remain so utterly detached. It was as if nothing had happened until it became real on television.

As we stepped out into the cold, my lingering

aversion to camcorders snapped into focus—I didn't want to record Matthew's and Emily's lives from behind a flickering black-and-white camcorder viewfinder. I would rather participate as a real flesh and blood father who laughs and claps and cries and remembers. The events in my kids' lives do not take on importance because they are recorded on video, they take on importance because they are important to someone—to me, their father.

So, if you happen to be near me whenever I hear Nat King Cole sing *Away in a Manger*, indulge me for a few minutes. In my heart I've recorded an important story to tell for a generation to come about how a cute little cow and a dapper young angel made Christmas all the more real to me.

Happy birthday to us

I was in the bathroom early one Sunday morning when Matthew caught me by surprise in the act. I hadn't anticipated anyone would be up at that hour, but there he was, having appeared as noiselessly as a kitten.

He didn't say anything, just rubbed his eyes and watched me curiously in the glow of the night light.

I turned back to the business at hand and kept right on going, writing a surprise note to my wife on the mirror with a piece of soap.

It was the least I could do. I couldn't afford diamonds or roses. But, at any rate, I had remembered.

Just as I finished, Janel walked down the hall toward the kitchen past the open bathroom door. Matthew stole out into the hall after her.

I went back to bed.

Moments later I heard Matthew taking care of his chores in the bathroom and then his voice piped up,

"What does the mirror say, Mama?"

"It says Happy Anniversary."

"What does anniversary mean?"

Rather than hearing her scoot him off to bed with a promise to explain later, as I might have done at such an hour, Janel began explaining in a warm, motherly tone, "It's a very special day, Matthew—"

My mind was one jump ahead of her, or so I thought, projecting an explanation of how this was Mama's and Papa's special day, a day for the two of them to go out and celebrate together, but as I heard Janel tuck Matthew back into bed, those weren't the words that came out of her mouth.

"An anniversary is the day we all celebrate our family's birthday."

"My birthday?"

"Well, sort of…," Janel answered slowly, obviously searching for more words. "Six years ago today your papa and I got married. That's when our family was born."

"Will we have a party?"

"That's a great idea, Matthew. Why don't you get some sleep now."

When Janel snuggled in next to me a minute later, I pretended to be asleep even though she'd closed and locked our bedroom door behind her. While touched by her explanation to Matthew, I was a hurt that she hadn't carved out the space for us to be alone later to celebrate our anniversary out on the town.

All the way to church later that morning I stewed that it probably hadn't been too smart to agree to get married two days after Christmas. Money would always be tight and it would never be easy for Janel and me to excuse ourselves from family activities during the holidays.

What had I been thinking when I said yes to that date six years ago?

What had Janel been thinking?

No answers had come by the time our priest began his sermon. Lost in my own thoughts, I hadn't paid much attention to the Scripture readings on this the Feast of the Holy Family.

Father Brendan began his homily with three questions:

1. If your children saw a TV show where teenagers kissed their parents goodnight, would they think it normal?

2. If you and your spouse were sitting in the same room reading, would your children come in just to be near you?

3. Have your children ever said, "I want to have a family just like ours"?

Janel's hand found mine across the pew and gave it a squeeze.

Without words, I knew she was proud; even though Matthew and Emily aren't teenagers, the buds of affirmative answers to all three questions had begun to open even then.

Mass went on, but I didn't hear much of it. With the squeeze of a hand my mind had found the answers it had been searching for.

Later, in the kitchen, Janel simply smiled when she found me baking a cake. When it was done, Matthew decorated it with six Gummy Bears, one for each year of our family's life. Janel then added four candles, one for each member of our family. With her leadership in a particularly rowdy version of *Happy Birthday*, with the words "to you" replaced with "to us," a family anniversary tradition was born.

I now see that six years before on our wedding day I had said "I do" to a lifelong relationship with the beautiful young bride at my side. Janel, on the other hand, had said "I do" to something much more bold— a lifelong commitment to nurturing a family that she could not yet see.

Nel, thanks for opening my eyes. And once again, for all time, I do.

Grandpa Elmer's bequest

Planning for vacation had been on our minds for a long time. But, as the sky darkened and our van rolled eastward into an intensifying snowstorm on I-80 near Des Moine too soon after Christmas, this was not how I had envisioned spending it.

"Why are we going to Illinois, Mama?" four-year-old Matthew had asked Janel earlier in the day at our first rest stop somewhere in Kansas.

"We've got to get to Grandpa Elmer's funeral," she had answered as I got out to fill the car with gas.

To my surprise, and distress, the fog that had been with us since Oklahoma City was freezing here in a thin sheet of ice that coated the gas pump. It wasn't yet freezing on the ground, but we still had 650 miles left to go—mostly north.

"Did Grandpa die?" Matthew asked as Janel carried him and two-year-old Emily toward the restroom.

"Yes, Matthew, he did."

"Oh," he said thoughtfully before the restroom door shut behind them.

For the rest of the trip as the fog turned into rain, then ice, and then into snow, and a 13-hour drive stretched into 14, 15, and then 16 hours, that two-letter response kept coming back to me, "Oh."

Even though I'd been part of Janel's family for a little over six years then, I'd barely become acquainted with her mother's father who everyone simply called Grandpa Elmer. Sad to say, but I did't even know the correct spelling of his last name.

If only I'd listened more carefully, paid more attention.

As the snow deepened and we exited the highway at Dixon, Illinois, I tried to remember what little I knew of Grandpa Elmer. He was a nice man. Quiet. He usually kept to himself at family gatherings. He never talked much. But, strangely, I never remember seeing an empty chair next to him. First it would be filled by this grandson, or that great granddaughter, or a son-in-law. Then a neighbor would drop in. You never knew who it might be, but the seat was always filled, though rarely did I hear Grandpa's voice.

What was it that drew them to Grandpa Elmer?

Late that night, our destination safely reached, I unloaded the van alone in the darkness. As melting snowflakes trickled down my neck in the stillness of that snowfilled night, an answer to my question came—people didn't flock to Grandpa Elmer because he talked, they came to him because he listened.

At his funeral a couple of days later, there were no tears, none at the cemetery and somebody wandering into the raucous family gathering later that evening would not have guessed that a death had brought this family together. Yet, beneath it all, they were taking Grandpa Elmer's death pretty hard, especially his forty-year-old grandson, David.

For whatever reason, preferring a bar in town to the company of his kin, David showed up late. While the other close family members huddled with an attorney who read the will in the living room, David pulled a chair up next to mine in a corner of the kitchen. He confided in me quietly as he surveyed the room. "Nobody here thinks I'm much on religion— and I'm not," he quickly added, stroking his scraggly beard. "I've been a pallbearer at any number of funerals, but, you know, this was the first time I'd ever been asked to ride in the hearse. I tell you what," he said, his clear blue eyes searching my face for some sign that I was listening, really listening, something that I was beginning to feel no one ever did for David except maybe for Grandpa. "That was the longest ride of my life. Being in that car with just the driver and Grandpa's body, now that did something to me. Some of these people here wouldn't believe it, but I did a lot of praying. I did."

With that, tears welled in his eyes and he left me. I wanted to stop him, listen longer, give him a hug, but I didn't.

Laying in bed that night, I thought about David. He was the black sheep of the family. Why had he chosen me to talk to? He and I are so totally different. I was just sitting quietly, minding my own business and he had just come up to me and—

At that moment it hit me that, in some mysterious way, even though it hadn't been mentioned in his will, maybe Grandpa had left me a more precious possession—a willingness to listen.

At that instant I wanted to protest. I certainly didn't feel worthy. I hadn't even listened to family members long enough to learn how to spell Granpa's last name.

My protests did me no good, though, because the longer I lay in bed thinking about that evening, the more deeply I found myself caring for David. It was then that I knew for certain, like it or not, I'd been given a gift that could not be returned.

So, Grandpa Elmer, thank you. I promise I'll try to do better, and I'll treasure the gift always.

❖

True professionals

Through an office window one afternoon, I saw my wife's van pulling into the parking lot at work. I hurried outside and my presence at the car door before she had even shut the motor off startled her.

"What are you doing here?" Janel mumbled, opening the door and pulling a Tootsie pop from her mouth.

"I figured it wouldn't do me any good to hide," I joked, handing over my paycheck for the bank deposit.

"Papa, look!" Emily called from inside the car.

I poked my head in the door and there sat Emily in the back seat, the loop of one of those doctor's office Saf-T-Pop suckers protruding from her lips. Her arms partially encircled a purple smiley-face balloon. A similar balloon bobbed near Matthew.

"Matthew went to the doctor," Emily said. "He was a good boy!"

Matthew had been running a fever for a few days and, after battling it with Tylenol, fluids, and sponge baths, Janel had finally decided it was time for a professional consultation.

Janel looked at me with a sheepish grin. "Are you ready for this?"

I shook my head, but she told me anyway.

"Ninety-one dollars," she said with a wince.

"You're kidding me!"

Janel shook her head. "The doctor said it's just a virus going around, but she took a culture just to be sure."

"No medicine?" I asked, incredulous that all $91 had bought was two twenty-five-cent suckers, two fifty-cent balloons, a sterile Q-tip and three-and-a-half minutes worth of a doctor's time.

"It's just a virus," Janel said.

"It's not a virus," I muttered, "it's more like a racket!"

"Hunh?" she said as I shut the car door to send them on their way. She rolled down the window for a goodbye kiss.

"Are you upset with me for taking him to the doctor?"

"No. I'm glad Matthew's OK, and I'm glad you'll sleep a little easier. I'm just in the wrong business, that's all."

Later, after I'd laid out my complaint, a co-worker

had chided me, "You should have talked to me first. I could have told you that was the most expensive clinic in town. I think they have a policy that no one gets out the door without lab work. They have their own lab, you know."

Other co-workers chimed in, sharing similar over-priced health care-related complaints. Most were far more expensive than mine. And, to be fair, there were stories of having received good care at the hands of competent professionals who had priced their services reasonably.

Unfortunately, too many of those good stories seemed to have taken place too many years ago.

At home that evening, I rocked with Matthew in the threadbare easy chair in our living room. His fever had abated somewhat, and we cuddled under an Indian-print blanket for the better part of three hours. As thoughts of the $91 bill came back, I grew upset that at my salary three hours wouldn't pay it.

I remembered a class in college where we'd discussed professions. The line dividing professions from occupations was that professionals, supposedly, render service without regard for the client's ability to pay.

Doesn't sound like the medical profession we'd experienced that day.

I finally carried Matthew to bed, wondering why I hadn't gone into an occupation worth several hundred dollars an hour. I had made good grades in school. I was smart enough. In recent years I'd even given thought to going back to school for a medical degree, but I'd stopped short when I thought of the time I'd be taking away from my family.

As I pulled the covers up to Matthew's chin and kissed him on the forehead, it came to me. Here, lying on this bed before me and the one next to it, were two small clients to whom every moment of my time is worth several hundred, if not thousands, of dollars. Their lives are in my hands. And, despite the value of services to be rendered over the next twenty years or so, it pleased me more than I can say to think that the totals at the bottom of Matthew's and Emily's imaginary bills will always read the same—"No charge."

I went to bed happy that night because, for $91, I had discovered that, as a father, I am truly a professional.

Don't tell them I can fly

The spring sunshine streaming in through the window one morning felt good on my face as I sat typing at my computer. My comfortable, wooden teacher's chair creaked when five-year-old Matthew crawled into my lap still rubbing his sleepy eyes. He was all dressed except for the pair of purple high-top sneakers he held in one hand. He sat very still, staring blankly at the computer screen for a moment before he spoke.

"When can I write my name on the computer, Papa?" he asked with a yawn as my fingers flew over the keys.

I heard him, but his question didn't register right away. I was concentrating on finishing some promotional literature which had to be done before I had to rush off to my day job.

"Not now, buddy," I finally responded. "I'm trying to print some letters to some newspapers."

"What kind of letters?"

"Letters that say 'Would you please buy some stories about my little boy Matthew and my little girl Emily,'" I said as I proofread the letter one last time.

Matthew perked up. "About us?" he asked, seemingly flattered.

"Yes, about you."

He thought for a moment. "Well," he began, "I guess it's OK, but don't tell them I can fly. They won't believe you."

Intrigued by his belief in some latent aerial abilities and touched by his concern for me that people wouldn't believe my words, I punched the key to send my letter to the printer on the table behind me. "So you don't think they would believe me?" I asked as I pulled on his shoes and tied them.

"No. Besides," he said, shrugging his shoulders, "I used to be able to fly a lot better, but now that I'm getting bigger, I can't fly as far."

The printer whirred and began spitting out letters. Matthew, apparently having forgotten his desire to write on the computer, slid off my lap, stretched out his arms and ran out the door. "Come on, Papa," I heard him call as he ran from room to room crowing joyfully like a rooster, "come fly with me."

Stuffing letters into envelopes seemed more important. As I worked, my mind was filled with visions of Matthew zooming through the air. But, as if pulled by some unseen force like a gravity that affects only adults, my thoughts soon turned back to practical things like paying taxes, coming up with a family budget, and trying to figure out how to keep everybody in clothes, food, and shelter for another year.

I forgot all about that morning until one weekend when we were visiting our friends on the farm in northwest Oklahoma. While I waited to attach an implement to John's tractor as he slowly backed toward me, I caught sight of Matthew and Emily on the porch getting acquainted with John's grandchildren. The rumble of the approaching tractor's engine drowned out their voices, but all of a sudden I saw Matthew stick his arms straight out at his sides and swoop down the steps. He looked back up at the porch and obviously said something. Immediately John's grandson, Alan, raised his arms and swooped down the steps, too. With outstretched arms they both cavorted out across the wheatfield.

My heart soared with them.

The next day, our visit over, we pulled out of the driveway. Emily and Janel waved goodbye, but Matthew was strangley silent. I jockeyed the rearview mirror to see his face. He stared out the window at the green wheat zipping along beside us. From the corner of his eye a tear rolled down his face.

"What's the matter, Matthew?" I asked.

He remained silent for a long moment before speaking, "I want to fly with my new friend Alan."

Now it was my turn to be silent. My adult under-standing of flying seemed totally inadequate. Appar-ently to Matthew it was not about being lighter than air, it was about making friends and believing there are no limits. As one grows older, more independent and increasingly consumed with cares of this world, it becomes increasingly difficult to fly.

So, whether you believe my words or not, it doesn't matter. In my own heart I know Matthew can fly.

So, now, if you'll excuse me, I've got to go find him. It's long past time I took another lesson and relearned a thing or two about flying.

Politicians just don't get it

I wasn't looking forward to the unpleasant problem Janel had warned me was awaiting my arrival at home one Friday. It had been festering all afternoon. She called me at work to tell me she was at wits end with our three-year-old and our five-year-old. One of them was lying to her about who had written in a school book with a magic marker.

It had gone past the usual "Not me" stage to include Matthew's introduction of incriminating evidence against Emily. Janel was withholding final judgment and pronouncement of sentence until my arrival.

One of the joys of fatherhood.

Not sure I had any more answers than she did, I took the long way home and drove slowly while listening to a recap of a spate of news conferences convened at the state capitol earlier in the afternoon.

News junkie that I am, I listened intently to a parade of public officials attempting to make hay of or exonerate themselves from the stinking sewage of wrongdoing in one more in a long string of Oklahoma's legendary political scandals. I grew increasingly disgusted with each renewed call (mostly from leniently-punished perpetrators) to "get this episode behind us and get on with the business of the state" as painlessly as possible.

To a man, they just didn't get it.

As a law-abiding citizen I was enraged not, as they seemed to be saying, that I had to pay for such a thorough criminal investigation with a cloud of suspicion cast over the entire state. Rather, I was livid that I had repeatedly been lied to by our governor. Time and again he'd publicly disavowed any knowledge of criminal activities. Only when faced with serious jail time on eight felony charges himself did he admit guilt before a judge in exchange for a slap on the wrist.

As I parked my pickup, the radio replayed the governor's refusal to answer one reporter's point-blank questions. His sidestepping screamed clearly that his actions hadn't been wrong because they were objectively wrong, they were wrong only because he'd been exposed and threatened with prosecution.

It was against this backdrop, moments later,

that I found myself sitting in judgment of my own children across our kitchen table. Their eyes avoided mine as I examined the evidence—a phonics book with scribbles of green across one page and a separate sheet of paper bearing similar markings.

"I'm disappointed," I began, "not because someone scribbled in a book, but because someone has lied." I waited until both Matthew's and Emily's eyes were fixed on mine. "I won't punish you for writing in the book, I just want to know the truth."

We stared at each other for a long moment before Matthew finally dropped his gaze to his lap and mumbled, "I did it."

His simple admission stung. As his father, I'd rather not have heard that. Not only had he done it, he'd gone so far as to manufacture false evidence to implicate his sister.

I reached over and gently lifted his chin until his gaze met mine.

"And you lied?"

He looked at me for a moment, his eyes flashing fire, his lower lip quivering. "Yes," he finally muttered, "I did." The sheer weight of his admission caused him to burst into tears.

At that moment I wanted to sweep him into my arms, to tell him that everything was all right, but, under the circumstances, I couldn't.

Punishment for lying and bearing false witness was fixed at the loss of television and Leggo priveleges.

His trial over, sentence pronounced, he slipped from his chair and made a run for the door. "One last thing," I found myself saying, catching him by the arm and turning him to face me, "I forgive you."

Still crying, he wordlessly scooped his Leggos off the coffee table and ran toward his room. A little while later he reappeared, his eyes dry.

I expected Matthew would steer clear of me for the rest of the weekend, but it didn't play out that way. Instead, without my asking, he stayed close to my side to offer a five-year-old's able assistance while I repaired and repainted the back door.

Something had obviously happened around our kitchen table by insisting on the truth and a little boy's payment for his mistakes.

Something good.

Something the politicians just don't get.

Hold you in my arms

It should have been a simple choice, but on such a picture-perfect fall Sunday afternoon in Dixon, Illinois, I didn't want to make it: I could either try to save the red kite I was teaching my nephew how to fly that was now diving toward the trees, or I could pick up my three-year-old daughter who was clamoring for attention at my knee. I couldn't do both. Holding a three-year-old is a two-handed job, as is trying to rescue a faltering kite.

So I gingerly tried to put Emily off with soothing words and a promise to pick her up momentarily while I frantically reeled in kite string that piled up rapidly at my feet.

"Papa, hold me please," she whined, clinging to my leg, her feet becoming entangled in the string.

"Just a minute, Em," I snapped, picking her up with one hand and shaking her loose from the string. She tripped when I set her down, collapsing in a sobbing heap.

Perturbed, I left Emily to fend for herself while I reeled in the kite. It couldn't have taken more than three minutes, but when I turned to pick her up, she was already gone.

I consoled myself with a couple of obvious thoughts: kids have to learn patience sometime and I didn't want my nephew's first kite-flying experience to end disastrously at the top of a seventy-foot elm tree. Then, almost as quickly as the incident had presented itself, I forgot about it.

Later that evening at a concert we'd been invited to at my mother-in-law's small town church hall, I was totally unprepared for what we found—it was packed. I'd never heard of guitarist and singer Tony Melendez, but apparently these people had. Except for a few scattered seats, it was standing room only. Janel settled with the kids in a couple of seats on the front row and I was left by myself a few rows back.

When Melendez appeared moments later, I was shocked: he had no arms.

With his guitar on the floor, his feet bare, a pick held between his toes, he proceeded to play better than many professionals I've heard who did have arms. For more than an hour he kept us spellbound with his singing and playing and speaking.

He told us what it was like to be born without

arms. He'd learned to do just about everything you or I could do, and obviously there were a few things he could do even better. But, despite his musical and financial success, tears came to his eyes when he explained there was one thing he longed to do, something he'd never be able to do, and it pained him deeply. He said he literally ached to hold his wife in his arms and a baby they prayed a miracle would make possible for them.

The crowd was hushed as he slowly began to play a song written for him by a spectator at one of his early concerts. *Hold You In My Arms* told the story of his longing and its accomplishment only in his dreams.

As the song went on, with tears in my own eyes, I realized I had made the wrong choice earlier in the day. In my desire to teach my nephew a good lesson about kite flying, I had missed the opportunity to teach him a greater lesson about life: holding a child is worth far more than three dollars worth of sticks and fabric.

Perhaps, a couple of dozen years hence, if I had chosen differently, my nephew would be setting aside a pressing project to pick up a child clamoring for attention at his own knee. "I can remember a fall day long ago," he'd say, "when my uncle let his kite crash into a tree just so he could hold his daughter in his arms. That's always stuck with me."

As I watched Melendez wipe his eyes on a towel draped over a microphone stand when the song was over, I found myself crushed that I couldn't bring the afternoon back, I couldn't change my decision.

Wiping away my own tears with a handkerchief, I was surprised to see Emily wriggling her way down the aisle toward me. I picked her up and set her in my lap. And then, as if she could read what had been going on in my mind and in my heart, she leaned her head against my shoulder, grabbed my hands and pulled my arms tightly across her chest.

My tears flowed again as I pondered the day's seemingly coincidental string of events and I thanked God for blessing me with this little girl, a second chance, and a mother-in-law's invitation to hear an extraordinary musician who had no arms.

A $500 lesson worth every penny

If someone had told me that a family trip to the dollar movies would actually cost $500, we never would have gone. Yet that's just what a trip to see Walt Disney's *Homeward Bound*, a story about two dogs and a cat struggling to complete a long trek home, cost us.

And, strange as it may sound, it was worth every penny.

It wasn't the movie that proved so expensive, but a chain of events set into motion at a park near the theater after the show. While the kids played on the slide in the twilight, a young calico kitten appeared from the shadows. Scrawny and weak, it appeared to have been abandoned.

"Papa, look!" three-year-old Emily shouted from her perch atop the slide. "A lost kitty!" She jumped down and grabbed it tightly around the middle, its legs dangling crazily as she ran over to show it to me. "Can we take her home, Papa?"

I intended to say no, I didn't want a cat in my house, but, you guessed it, I couldn't say no.

An ad in the local newspaper brought no takers and the kids grew more attached to her as the weeks passed. Five-year-old Matthew had christened her "Whiskers" at the vet's office during a checkup.

Unfortunately for the kids, the vet's report wasn't good. He could rid the cat of a pesky parasite problem, but a digestive disorder that caused her to have constant diarrhea might be incurable.

Janel and I discussed it that night and I found myself advocating putting the cat to sleep. It would be best for the cat, I argued. Deep inside, though, I wondered if it simply wouldn't be best for me.

I was surprised when Janel called me at work a couple of days later and said the cat appeared to be getting better. She also said that she had made a deal with a pet shop to find the cat a new home. To get the kids to agree, however, she'd had to promise that we'd take the cat back in three weeks if she had no new home.

That Saturday they loaded the cat into the car and that was that, or so I thought. Thirty minutes later a phone call brought me in from the garage.

"Jim, there's been a little accident," Janel's sheepish voice said. "Everybody's OK. The car's driveable and we should be home soon."

"You what?" I growled in disbelief.

"We had an accident pulling out of the pet shop. I'll talk to you later."

Instantly the cost of the trip to the dollar movies—and the cat—had skyrocketed to $500, the amount of our insurance deductible.

Like a boomerang, the cat did indeed come back to our home three weeks later. Kittens sell. Cats don't.

Matthew rechristened her "Cuddles" for her gentle manner and I tried to make peace with the realization that I was now owned by a cat. It was working until the afternoon I discovered the large wet spot reeking of cat urine on our bed.

I was ready to call the pound her new home.

Janel called some friends with a farm, and found "Puddles" a new home two hundred miles away.

The kids were still a little sad when they returned from their trip to drop her off, but their moods brightened a couple of days later when our friends from the farm called us. They said the cat and their Collie, Sandy, had become friends, often curling up together to sleep.

"Looks like Cuddles found the best home, guys," I said, hanging up the phone.

"No she didn't, Papa," Matthew corrected, "we have the best home."

My heart melted at his innocent perception that as a family, somehow, we're doing something right.

A couple of days later, still touched by my five-year-old's vision, I bought him and Emily a present. Perhaps each time we watch their video of *Homeward Bound* they'll remember something of the $500 lesson about home and family that Matthew translated into words for us.

I know I will.

I'd love to go to lunch, but...

Six dollars. Not a king's ransom mind you, but I was a little surprised to find that much in my wallet as I dressed for work one morning. I guess it had been there since pay day. I was amazed it was still there. Immediately my mind began thinking of ways to spend it.

Six dollars isn't enough to buy Janel and me movie tickets and popcorn even at the dollar movies, so I forgot that idea. Legos for Matthew or a Breyer horse figure for Emily were out—too expensive.

So, obviously, the only logical way to spend it was on myself.

I had refused a lot of offers from friends at work to go to lunch recently, so maybe there was the answer. I'd simply look somebody up and we'd "do" lunch—cheaply, of course.

A co-worker from back east had asked me once why we Okies put so much stock in lunch. Apparently in his corner of the world lunch is little more than a pit stop to fill up the tank.

"This is Oklahoma," I explained. We do business in the coffee shop, in the diner, over lunch, at the dinner table. For some reason, that's just the way it is. Maybe it's a little easier for us to swallow the details of a business deal along with a cup of coffee or a chicken-fried steak. I think it has something to do with looking someone in the eye and getting a feel for him as a person. Maybe it's biblical. Maybe we think it's a little tougher to get cheated by someone you've broken bread with.

At any rate, as I dispensed goodbye kisses to Matthew and Janel who were eating breakfast in the kitchen, that's how I intended to spend my six dollars that day. I found Emily still sleeping in her bed and kissed her softly on the cheek. "Goodbye, Sweet Pea. I love you."

Like a flower bud turning to greet the rising sun, she turned her face toward mine and stretched her arms around my neck. "Come home for lunch, Papa?" she yawned. "Please?"

Stubborn as I am, I didn't want to let go of the plans I'd already laid for lunch in my mind. But somehow I couldn't flat out refuse such a sweet offer from my three-year-old, either.

So, I did the next best thing. "We'll see," I responded evasively, avoiding a promise. No sooner had the words escaped my lips than the self-deprecation began. Why couldn't I have just told her no instead of trying to weasle my way out?

In the bustle of problems that presented themselves at work that morning, I soon forgot my distress at deceiving a three-year-old. It wasn't until one of our department directors caught me in the parking lot at noon and asked me if I had made plans for lunch that I realized I'd forgotten to carry through on my own desires. I hadn't asked anyone out to lunch. Here was my chance.

"Funny you should ask..." I responded, only to discover the words that came out next didn't match my earlier intentions, "...but I do have plans. I'm going home. I have lunch with my family."

Her reply was equally surprising, "That's neat!" she said, getting into her car. "That's neat."

I climbed into my pickup, not so sure that it was. Somewhere in the recesses of my mind I still harbored the image of myself as an astute, ladder-climbing public relations man who conducted business wherever he can find it—especially at lunch.

Wheeling into the driveway at home, perhaps my choice to eat with my family shouldn't have come as a surprise in light of the phone conversation I'd had the previous afternoon. It was with my former boss, a man whom I admire deeply. Nearing retirement, a recent brush with serious illness had given him pause to consider his life and how he'd spent it thus far.

Somewhere along the line he'd detoured from the path that leads to the executive suite, choosing instead a path closer to home. Each day that choice included sharing lunch with his wife and kids, a time which they carefully protected.

For that choice, he bore no regret.

When we parted company nearly three years before, unbeknownst to him, I carried his legacy with me. Janel and I bought a home near my new job just so I could eat lunch at home with her and the kids. And, despite the images lingering in my head, on most days at noon, that's where you'd find me. Exactly where I needed to be.

So, John, I owe you one. My family owes you one. Some day when we're up in your neck of the woods again, I'll take you to lunch. I will. Better yet, let's make it dinner—we both have other plans for lunch.

All the world needs a waver

After what she caught me doing one afternoon, the UPS lady who served our neighborhood probably thought I was fresh, daft, or a little of both.

I had been heading back to work after having come home for lunch and was stopped at the stop sign at the end of our block. Listening to the radio, I hadn't noticed her truck slip up behind my pickup. My left hand was thrust out the window waving frantically when I caught sight of her in my rearview mirror.

She looked at me quizzically. Then, as if to go along with some flirtatious little game I was playing, waved tentatively back at me.

Embarrassed, I almost stopped waving, but, remembering the promise three-year-old Emily had extracted from me moments before, I kept right on.

"Papa, wave all the way down the block, OK?" she had asked repeatedly as I handed her to my wife as I had climbed into my pickup.

"Sure, Emily. I promise," I had said.

Now here I was, waving like a wildman, traffic whizzing past in front of me, unable to pull away and end this silly affair.

I glanced back at the UPS lady. She caught me looking at her and waved once again.

I shrunk down in my seat with a chuckle, but true to my promise, I kept waving.

The traffic finally cleared and I was able to pull away from the stop sign. I looked back over my shoulder to see Emily, Matthew and Janel, who had been standing on our porch waving at me, disappear from sight.

Thankful the escapade was over, I pulled my hand back in the window and went on my way.

The UPS lady isn't the only one who has caught me "waving all the way down the block."

Neighborhood drivers have subjected me to strange looks. School children waiting for their buses in the morning now largely ignore the weird man in the brown pickup who can't seem to stop waving.

It's a little game I began playing with Matthew when we moved into our present home a little over a year-and-a-half before. What with the move and all, he had been afraid I was going to leave him and never come back. Janel brought him outside to wave to me as I drove off to work the following morning.

What began as a way to calm a four-year-old boy's

fears turned into a daily ritual that Emily picked up and continued on with. It seemed she developed some sixth sense that could determine when I was leaving the house, even when she was in a deep sleep. She would appear, as if on cue, every morning to rally Matthew and Janel to come wave.

That is until one Tuesday morning when I found myself climbing into my pickup after having eaten breakfast with no sign of Emily, Matthew or Janel. I put the key in the ignition and paused a moment, waiting hopefully for the front door to open and Emily's smiling face to appear.

It never did.

As I drove off, I looked back but saw no signs of motion on our porch. At the stop sign, I waved anyway to a little girl waiting for the school bus before turning the corner.

All the rest of the day I pretended not to care, rationalizing that kids grow up, change, and don't need the same reassurances they once did.

For some reason as I walked to my truck at quitting time, the memory of a retarded man who lived in our neighborhood in Oklahoma City came to mind. He used to stand at the intersection of 19th and 23rd streets waving to traffic. Day in and day out he would be there smiling and waving when I drove to work at Safeway after school. Some motorists returned his wave. Most did not.

I was in the most did not category until I saw a Chevy loaded with teenagers about my age gesturing and yelling obscenely as they raced past him one day.

The Waver smiled and waved just the same.

As I neared home that afternoon, Janel and the kids were in the yard planting flowers. When they caught sight of my truck they began waving wildly as if to make up for their absence that morning.

It did my heart good. For even if my family doesn't need the reassurances they once did, I do, because after that one afternoon in Oklahoma City, I'll always be a waver.

TV can do without me

Engrossed in an episode of the news program *48 Hours* about missing children one night, I pretended not to hear when Matthew called to me from his bedroom.

"Papa!" Receiving no answer, he waited for a moment and tried again, his tone a little softer this time. "Papa?"

I was riveted to the television by the anguished cries of a mother pleading for the safe return of her teenage daughter.

"Papa, I need you," Matthew called out again.

Annoyed, I waited for a commercial before walking down the hall to his room. "What do you need?"

"Will you come snuggle?" he asked dreamily, his eyelids heavy with fatigue.

His request caught me by surprise—he doesn't often ask me to snuggle. I heard the theme music for the show coming back on in the living room. I felt drawn to return to the television and I found myself rationalizing that Matthew was now five years old—plenty old enough to sleep by himself. Still, a sense of guilt prompted me to refrain from turning him down flatly. "Just a minute, Matthew. I'll be back."

Back in the living room, the trials of a family waiting for word of the missing girl they knew as granddaughter, daughter, sister, niece, and cousin played out on the screen. Each time their phone rang an expectant hush fell over the house. Each time their hopes were dashed.

Matthew called again, this time his voice weaker than before.

As the last few minutes of the show were playing out with obviously no happy ending in sight, I kept watching. I knew Matthew wouldn't be awake long, but again, my response was, "Just a minute."

When the program finally ended I hustled back toward the kids' room. I planned to snuggle for a couple of minutes and then it would be back to the living room to watch the news.

Too late. Matthew was already asleep. As I spread a blanket over him, a sense of remorse at not having honored his request seized me—I'd let my own son down just to watch a few minutes of television.

I crawled into his bed anyway, my long legs sticking out over the end. I snuggled close and kissed him. I told him I was sorry. I wondered if sleep were like surgery; doctors now think that even though a patient is anesthetized, he can still hear.

Lying there with him in bed that night, I confessed that sometimes I'm often not the father I'd hoped I would be. I work too much. I worry too much. I waste too much time.

As I began to grow tired myself, memories of life on the farm filtered in. Living outside of Alva, we didn't have cable. A satellite dish was too expensive. Our small antenna could only pick up the public television station. Everything else was snow. Instead of watching TV, Janel, Matthew, Emily and I took bike rides down country roads or played outside in the evenings, or worked in the garden.

Together.

I began to feel a sense of powerlessness come crushing down. With such easy access to television I had found it ever so easy to begin denying my children access to the only thing they really ever want from me, their father—my time.

The longer I thought about it the worse I felt. I felt like an alcoholic or a drug addict. Even though I did't watch television often, once I sat down in front of it, I was hooked, the evening was shot.

Since I began watching television after our move, a new phrase had crept into my vocabulary: "Just a minute." Visions of that phrase as my epitaph filled my head.

I crawled out of Matthew's bed to leave, and despite

what had just gone on in my mind, like the addict I had become, I headed back to the tube.

I paused in front of the television and flipped through the channels, settling on "The Tonight Show." I stood there watching Jay Leno much the way a bachelor stands in front of the refrigerator grazing.

Jay had me hooked.

From down the hall I heard Emily's small voice, "Papa 'nuggle?"

I stood there indecisively for a moment before, as if helped by some unseen power, without thinking, I finally found my hand clicking the television off.

Warmed by my restored ability to choose, I called quietly on my way down the darkened hall, "I'm coming, Em."

The television will just have to learn to get along without me again.

The road not taken

The conversation I found myself entangled in at work late one August afternoon was more than a little awkward. On my way to the FAX machine I had stumbled into a group of co-workers who were trading stories about the difficulty of finding school supplies for their children on the eve of the first day of school.

"What about you?" one friend had asked, politely including me in the conversation. "Matthew will be in kindergarten this year, won't he?"

"He's old enough," I parried, avoiding a direct answer. A growing tightness in the pit of my stomach warned me to get out without sending my FAX before I found myself verbally cornered.

"You enrolled him didn't you?" another fellow employee asked pointedly as if she were an attorney boring in for a straight answer.

"I remember seeing a notice about it in the paper back in the spring..."

With everyone staring at me as I fumbled for more words, like a fish in a net, I was caught. There was no backing out. For the first time in front of my education peers, I had to spill the beans: "We're... we're homeschooling," I stuttered.

I expected to be skewered on the spot. I thought I'd be branded a fundamentalist kook who wanted to shelter his kids from reality. I never would have expected the reaction I got, though.

"Well, I suppose you could do that," a teacher friend finally responded in a nonjudgmental yet nonsupportive kind of way.

The others responded with a simple "oh" or a blank stare. I took it to mean that my wife's and my decision was at least a little on the distastefully eccentric side for them.

Rather than press for more information, though, they then proceeded to try and sell me on the merits of the local school system's kindergarten program, which did indeed sound very good.

The decision which Janel and I had made, which I had thought was firm, was beginning to soften— at least in my mind.

"They test the kids before they place them in classes and group them by ability," one of them said. "It's a fairly sophisticated system."

When I got home that evening, instead of watching the news, I sat down with Janel in the kitchen.

"I don't know, Nel," I said. "The school system here sounds pretty good. Maybe we should reconsider."

"I thought we agreed my individual attention would be best for the kids." Janel thumped the box of school books and lesson plans that sat in the middle of the kitchen table. "I wish for once you'd make a decision and just stick with it. We'll do just fine, Jim," she reassured.

It was an odd conversation. Just a few months before it had been me reassuring her over the same kitchen table that homeschooling was the way to go. I'd checked out all kinds of books on the subject. I'd talked with Janel's sister who has successfully taught three kids of her own. I did everything I could to understand what was involved and what it would take to do the job right.

And now, as things had come full circle, I was the one who wasn't sure. And I couldn't quite put my finger on why. Janel had taught at the University of Missouri. I've taught at three colleges. What could I have been worried about?

The decision stood and the first day of school came and went. Matthew started his formal lessons at home and yet I still didn't feel settled.

My mother called that evening and asked about her grandchild's first day of school. Without hesitation I told her the truth, fully expecting a grilling. She and Dad had sacrificed all their lives to send us kids to private schools. A long pause preceded her answer.

"That sounds great, Jim. I really think you guys are doing the right thing for the kids."

In that moment it became clear that doing the right thing sometimes means diverging from the beaten path, like in Robert Frost's poem *The Road Not Taken.*

My problem was that I wanted to see farther down the path before admitting my choice. As I hung up the phone, the certainty grew that with the loving traveling companions of family, I don't have a thing to worry about because all our choices made together, made with love, truly will make all the difference.

True home improvements

I probably should have kept my mouth shut, but I just couldn't resist. I had stopped by my dad's office one afternoon and he had asked me how my in-laws' visit to our house was going.

"To tell you the truth, Dad, I wish there were some way to get them to stay longer," I had said. "Janel's dad is just about finished with his remodel job on our bathroom. Yesterday afternoon we replaced the rusted-out floorboard in the pickup, and there's a whole list of things we could probably tackle with a little more time."

Somewhere in the middle of my recitation of projects Gordy and I had undertaken, my dad had dropped his gaze back to the stack of checks on his desk he'd been signing when I entered. "Sounds like you guys have been busy," he said without looking up.

"I'll say," I said, pulling a chair up in front of his desk. I was excited. Janel's folks had been with us for the better part of two weeks, and her father and

I were having a lot of fun working on projects together.

My dad thumbed through his stack of checks
rapidly, the way a bank teller does when she's
counting money, until he found one he'd missed. In
his ornate fashion, he signed his signature and
returned to thumbing through the rest of the stack.

"I don't think there's anything Janel's dad can't
fix," I continued. "You know what?" I asked, leaning
forward in my chair to try and draw Dad's attention
away from his work. "Why, when Gordy needed a
bench grinder to fix something the other day, he just
went out and bought one. And instead of packing it
up to take home with him, he just told me to keep it."

When my dad finally looked up at me, it appeared
as if he'd grown weary somehow in the short span of
time I'd been with him that afternoon.

"Your father-in-law sounds like quite a guy."

From his facial expression and tone of voice, it was
clear I'd crossed some invisible line that a son is never
to cross when bragging on his father-in-law. It was
all I could do to bring the conversation to a close and
make a graceful exit.

It wasn't until I was in the car heading back home
a little while later that I recalled a phone call I'd made
to my father two years earlier, shortly after Janel and
I had bought the house we were living in. I had come
home one evening to find a new tile floor in the master

bathroom and a bill for materials on the kitchen table. I recall complaining to my dad over the phone that my father-in-law, who had come to help us move, had busied himself repairing and replacing things around the house for Janel while I was away at work.

After my father stopped laughing, his advice had simply been, "Just keep your mouth shut. You don't know how good you've got it—"

"But, Dad—"

"He's her father, Jim. And it's her house too. There will always be more work than you can keep up with anyway."

Even though I felt he didn't understand, I had taken his advice at the time. It went down hard. But as I pulled into the drive that afternoon after having visited with my father only to find Gordy cutting a piece of trim on the table saw in my garage, I found it much easier to believe that there was indeed more work around the house than one person can keep up with.

When I had changed into my grubbies and went to work next to Janel's father that evening, I felt out of sorts. I felt that way until it finally occurred to me that my dad must have felt like a divorced father whose son had come to visit earlier that afternoon. Instead of acknowledging his father's continued love and concern, the son couldn't stop talking about the latest trinket his stepfather had bestowed on him.

It must have hurt my father deeply.

It wasn't until after Gordy and Irene had left a few days later that it all began to make sense. As I swept up the mess we'd left in the garage, the familiar aroma of pine wafted up from the sawdust piled on the floor. It was the same aroma of many a childhood Saturday afternoon spent in my father's workshop, at my father's side, as he labored to build new cabinets for our kitchen, or construct a bookshelf for the living room, or craft a hutch to hold the china in the dining room he'd added onto our house. Immediately I felt a sense of peace, a sense of being at home, of being loved.

It was then that I knew, without a doubt, that I liked working with Gordy so much because he reminds me of my father. Neither of them say "I love you" with words, they say it in deeds.

And so, Dad, as much as I've grown to love him, Gordy will never be my father; no one can ever take your place.

And, believe me, every time Matthew or Emily climbs up on the stool next to me at my workbench, I'll remember our past. And, most of all, I'll remember that you love me.

❖

Bless me with a lullaby

I've begun to notice lately that it's been particularly quiet at the Apel house—too quiet. A visitor to our home probably wouldn't notice at all; the air is usually filled with the typical noises one would expect when living in close proximity to a four-year-old and a six-year-old—the whooping, the screaming, the shrieks of playful laughter mixed with the numbing chatter emanating from computerized toys. But, on balance, its been very quiet.

The silence becomes particularly noticeable, and, lately, uncomfortable, at about 8:30 every evening. The kids' teeth have been brushed, Janel has led them off to bed, and it's the time when I get a few minutes to myself. I like to turn off the television, settle into the recliner in the living room, and pick up a book. For the last couple of weeks, though, instead of opening the book, I've found myself just sitting. I'll sit with my eyes shut, my ears straining for the lilting notes of my wife's voice.

Unfortunately, the only place I've heard the sweet music I'm listening for lately has been in my own mind. The kids no longer like Janel to sing them lullabies at bed time—they say they're too big for them—but I sure do miss them.

To be honest, I hadn't really thought about all this until someone put something they had found at the office Xerox machine on my desk a couple of weeks back. It was the jacket copy from a cassette tape of lullabies by Michael Card. My co-worker said she'd read it and assumed it belonged to me. No, it didn't, but after reading it, I wished it did.

The jacket said that lullabies come around three times in a lifetime. When we are babies our parents sing them to us, if we are fortunate. When we are parents, if we are smart, we sing them to our children. Then, if we are blessed to be grandparents, we have the opportunity to sing them once again to those whose little faces remind us of those we have loved all our lives.

As I sat at my desk and thought about it, I concluded I hadn't been very wise. I couldn't remember many times when I'd sung lullabies to Matthew and Emily. I was away from home a lot with graduate school and all. On nights when I was home, mostly I just hummed the kids to sleep because I didn't sing lullabies often enough to remember many of the words.

For all my education I can recite the first twenty lines of Chaucer's *Canterbury Tales*, but I know not an entire lullaby. Sitting at my desk thinking, it occurred to me that is not something a person who fancies himself to be a pretty good father should be particularly proud of.

A couple of days later I was having lunch with my brother, Tom. He's a good friend of mine. Usually we talk business. His business. My business. How we might do more business together. From out of the blue in the middle of a bite of barbecued beef sandwich he asked, "Are you guys thinking about having more kids?"

Reflexively I found myself saying, "No, we really haven't thought about it much."

Tom let it drop, but my mind didn't. At home later that evening, about 8:30 to be exact, as I settled into my recliner I found myself listening once again.

All at once, as if I'd barely caught myself from falling backwards in a chair at the dinner table after having been warned not to tip it back, I realized I'd lied to my brother—I'd thought about having more children a lot.

It seems I can't look at our daughter Emily or our son Matthew anymore without thinking, "Wouldn't it be nice..." And there simply are no words to describe the longing for another child I feel whenever I take Janel in my arms when we are alone.

Too many times, though, I have been guilty of dismissing such thoughts for fear of the future that I cannot see. I don't worry so much about the political or financial future, but I do worry about a future for my children of which I am not a part. Always in the back of my mind is the legacy of my father's father who died when his children were very young.

How does one get over a fear like that?

I don't have the answer yet, but, for my part, I am trying my best to learn the words to those lullabies.

Acknowledgments

Thank you for reading SMALL VOICES. I hope it has been as enjoyable for you to read as it has been for me to write.

I wish to thank all those who have touched my life and have graciously allowed me to include them in my columns and in this book. My life has been changed forever and I will be forever in their debt.

I owe special thanks to my brothers, Tom and Chris, whose assistance, support, advice and encouragement make possible my vocation as a writer in this technological twentieth century.

To the readers of my weekly column who have shared with me their own stories, words of encouragement, and occasional (albeit well-deserved) admonishments, I remain especially grateful.

Thank you all ever so much.

About the author

At one time or another, Jim Apel has earned his keep as a television news photographer, radio announcer, public relations director, journalism teacher, freelance photographer, farmer, sports writer and airport lineboy. His work as a journalist has been recognized for its excellence by the National Newspaper Association and the Associated Press.

Apel is currently a columnist and author living outside of Guthrie, Oklahoma.

Order form

Additional copies of SMALL VOICES are available directly from the publisher at $8.95 each plus $2 shipping per copy. On orders of five or more books, *Sparrow Press* will pay all shipping costs. Satisfaction is guaranteed—you may return any books for a full refund.

❖

Please send _____ copies of SMALL VOICES to:

Name _____

Address _____

City _____ State _____ Zip _____

Phone _____

Enclosed is my check or money order in the amount of $_____.

Mail orders to:

Center 3000, Suite 239
3000 United Founders Blvd.
Oklahoma City, OK 73112